JERU'S JOURNEY

The Hal Leonard Jazz Biography Series

JERU'S JOURNEY

The Life and Music of Gerry Mulligan

SANFORD JOSEPHSON

Hal Leonard Books

An Imprint of Hal Leonard Corporation

Published in 2015 by Hal Leonard Books
An Imprint of Hal Leonard Corporation
7777 West Bluemound Road
Milwaukee, WI 53213

Trade Book Division Editorial Offices
33 Plymouth St., Montclair, NJ 07042

Printed in the United States of America

Book design by Michael Kellner

Library of Congress Cataloging-in-Publication Data

Josephson, Sanford.
Jeru's journey: the life and music of Gerry Mulligan / Sanford Josephson.
pages cm
Includes bibliographical references and index.
ISBN 978-1-4803-6024-2 (pbk.)
1. Mulligan, Gerry. 2. Jazz musicians--United States--Biography. 3. Saxophonists--United States--Biography. 4. Composers--United States--Biography. I. Title.
ML419.M79J67 2015
788.7'165092--dc23
[B]

2015019654

www.halleonardbooks.com

This book is dedicated to my grandson, Riley. He loves his music.

Contents

Introduction

Sanford Josephson

"Gerry Mulligan is one of the truly unique figures in American music, not just speaking of jazz, but of music in a broader, general way."

—Jon Newsom, retired chief of the Music Division, Library of Congress

That quote by Jon Newsom, from the video documentary *Listen: Gerry Mulligan*, perfectly describes the basis and motivation for this book, which chronicles Mulligan's enormous contributions to jazz and American music as a composer, arranger, bandleader, and baritone saxophonist. Thanks to Franca Mulligan, Gerry's widow and partner for more than twenty-two years, I received access to his recorded autobiography, *Jeru: In the Words of Gerry Mulligan* (by Gerry Mulligan with Ken Poston). I have also quoted heavily from *Listen: Gerry Mulligan*.

That material has been supplemented by more than forty interviews with those who knew Mulligan and played with him, as well as with others who were influenced by him. I have also drawn on many articles, reviews, and excerpts from books, helped greatly by the resources of the Institute of Jazz Studies at Rutgers University–Newark, the Jazzinstitut Darmstadt in Darmstadt, Germany, and the Music Division of the Library of Congress. This book could not have been completed, however, without the indispensible assistance and guidance of my most trusted editor—my wife, Linda.

Introduction

My passion for jazz began developing in the mid-1960s when I spent two years in Japan, working in the public information office of the American Red Cross's Far Eastern Area headquarters. I remember buying *Gerry Mulligan '63: The Concert Jazz Band* in the Army PX and wearing it out on my turntable. But it was not until I moved to New York in 1968 and was able to see Mulligan in person that I was able to enjoy the fruits of his musical genius. I saw him several times in a variety of settings—concerts at Carnegie Hall and Lincoln Center, and many times at clubs, primarily at Hopper's in Greenwich Village and StoryTowne on East 58th Street.

In 1981, I interviewed him at his home in Darien, Connecticut, for a newspaper article that became the basis for a chapter in my previous book, *Jazz Notes: Interviews Across the Generations*.

The following pages trace Mulligan's life and career from his early days of arranging for big bands to the end of his life, when he was revered and recognized as a major composer, arranger, bandleader, and baritone saxophonist whose influence spread beyond the world of jazz.

Mulligan once said that he aimed for 42nd Street and ended up on 52nd Street. That is an indirect way of pointing out that practically everything he wrote, arranged, and played had a sense of melody at its core.

All quotations from Gerry Mulligan, unless otherwise noted, are from *Jeru: In the Words of Gerry Mulligan*, by Gerry Mulligan with Ken Poston.

1

'A GREAT GUY, A BORN GENIUS'

Johnny Warrington was the leader of a thirty-piece orchestra that played on Philadelphia radio station WCAU in the early 1940s. He also wrote many of the stock arrangements that music publishers sold during that period. But he never achieved fame or even widespread recognition among the general public and would be just a footnote in the history of the big-band era if not for a chance encounter with a sixteen-year-old named Gerry Mulligan. Mulligan, a student at West Philadelphia Catholic High School, approached Warrington and said, "I'd like to write for your band.'"

Mulligan remembered Warrington's reaction. "He laughed and said, 'Why not?' Then he assigned some tune for me to do, so I took it and wrote an arrangement. He went over it with me, went through the chart with me, made suggestions, and asked me to rewrite it and bring it back. A couple of weeks later, he bought it and assigned another piece. That was the beginning of my professional career as an arranger. He was more of an arranging teacher than I'd ever had before or have had since. I've always thought what it would have been like to be Johnny Warrington and have this kid show up and say, 'I'd like to write for your band.'"

Warrington had no way of knowing that Mulligan would go on to become a brilliant arranger, composer, performer, and bandleader, but he did recognize that there was something special about the boy. Elliot Lawrence, a bandleader Mulligan would eventually arrange for at WCAU a couple of years later, recalled receiving a phone call from Warrington: "He told me, 'This young guy's got talent.'"

Philadelphia was the last stop in a childhood that had taken Mulligan from his birthplace in Queens Village, New York, to Marion, Ohio, to Chicago, to Kalamazoo, Michigan, to Detroit and then Reading, Pennsylvania. His father, George Mulligan, an engineer, had taken a job in New York with a maritime company, moving the family from Chester, Pennsylvania, where Gerry's three older brothers had been born. "One of my mother's favorite stories," Mulligan said, "was about the day I was born—April 6, 1927. Since I was the fourth child, she felt she knew pretty well what was going on. Apparently, it was an easy pregnancy, and she said to my father one morning when he was getting ready to go to work, 'I think today's the day.' She called the doctor, and the doctor came over and examined her and said, 'I don't think so' and took off." Shortly after the doctor left, the baby started coming out, and Louise Mulligan had to call a neighborhood midwife for assistance. "I was born in the kitchen," Mulligan said, "and apparently I lifted my head and looked around. She loved that. I amended that story by adding to it. I always said that I took a look around and decided to get back in. I've been trying to get back in all my life."

When Mulligan was less than a year old, the family moved to Marion, about forty miles north of Columbus, so that his father could accept an executive position with the Marion Power Shovel Company. Mulligan's early memories of life in Marion were of an African-American woman named Lily Rowan, whom his mother had hired as a helper. "She was kind of a nanny to me. I became her 'baby.' She was very protective of me. When I got older, I remembered some of these things. My father could be a pretty stern fellow, not given much to a sense of humor, and he had some very authoritarian kinds of rules. I guess I was not eating something I should have been eating, and he said, 'By God, you're supposed to be eating everything on your plate.' I don't know if he smacked me or what, but Lily came flying in from the kitchen and said, 'Don't you hit my bonzo.' It's funny. My relationship with Lily seemed perfectly normal to me, but it must have seemed to my brothers like I was really spoiled, to have a protector and a woman who was so warmhearted and outgoing. She literally adopted me."

Marion was an industrial city of about thirty thousand people. A twelve-piece band still played in the pit in the city's Palace Theater after the movies, and live music was available in other places, as well. Mulligan's first recollection of going to the Palace was of the big band in the pit. "In the days of the silent movies," he explained, "the movies were accompanied by a score and parts for a symphony orchestra. That was the difference between the big movie houses and the B and C theaters. It was kind of a sidelight of the period, but those insights were important to me, to be able to compare what the atmosphere for the music was like in that period."

Mulligan spent a lot of time at Lily's house, which had a player piano. "I used to love that," he said, "playing Fats Waller rolls and all sorts of things. I would lean against the piano bench, nose at keyboard height, pumping away. Spending as much time as I did in the black part of town, I just thought that was the normal way things were. I learned things about the community there that were totally different from the rest of town. For instance, when the various black bands would come through, there were no hotels for them. So, the community would put them up. Often there would be musicians staying at Lily's house."

With the emergence of radio, the big bands started to gain in popularity in the 1930s, and bandleaders such as Benny Goodman, Tommy Dorsey, and Duke Ellington became the equivalents of today's superstars. "They were my heroes." Mulligan said. "They were not just musicians; they were like movie stars. So they started putting bands into the theaters because they were drawing people, even though it was primarily dance music. And later the bands brought singers. Sinatra and Dick Haymes came out of the bands."

All of this was developing as the Mulligan family moved out of Marion in 1937, when Gerry was ten. After a brief stay in New Jersey while his father was working on a special project in Puerto Rico, the family moved to Chicago for his father's latest job. "That had the advantage of being a very active city where music was concerned," Mulligan said. "My brother Phil and I would be off to the theaters all the time to hear the bands. Four or five theaters in Chicago played name bands. I had heard Louis Armstrong on the radio and saw him in the movies. But unless he came to a theater, I couldn't see him, because I was too young to go to the clubs."

After a year in Chicago, the family moved to Kalamazoo, Michigan, where Mulligan was inspired by a neighbor to take up the trumpet. "We lived in a kind of suburban area," Mulligan recalled, "and the kid across the street, Jimmy Shoemaker, played a good trumpet, flashy stuff like 'Carnival of Venice' and 'Flight of the Bumblebee.' That really gave me the desire to play a horn." Mulligan was enrolled in a Catholic school in downtown Kalamazoo, and "during recess, the Michigan Central and New York Central luxury trains would go by, and I'd see people sitting with the white tablecloths and silverware and say, 'Oh, man, what am I doing here?' That was my idea of heaven."

The following year, inspired by a new music program at his school, Mulligan switched from trumpet to clarinet and became part of a makeshift band that consisted of his clarinet, one trumpet, one violin, a piano, and drums. "I had the desire to write something for us. That was my first arrangement. I was fascinated with the tune "Lover" with its chromatic progression. So I sat down and tried to write out an arrangement of "Lover"—lots of whole notes and quarter notes, trying to get all the moving parts and all that stuff. I ultimately never heard it, because the school was taught by nuns and, like a fool, I put on top of all the sheets the title, "Lover"—and the nuns took one look at the title, and that was the end of that."

Next stop was Detroit. "My father," Mulligan recalled, "had a dream that all of his sons would become engineers. My two older brothers were in high school, and my father would put them into college if they would go to engineering school. If they didn't want to go into engineering school, they would have to shift for themselves. They knuckled under. My father never discussed education with me. Maybe it was because he knew what I wanted. I wanted to go to music school. I had taken piano lessons in the second grade in Marion. At the first recital, I forgot the piece halfway through. I was taken off the stage, and the nun told my mother, 'Save your money. He'll never learn how to play this stuff the way it's written.'"

On December 7, 1941, Mulligan was in a Detroit theater listening to the Erskine Hawkins band play "After Hour Blues." "I came out of the theater," he said, "and the country was at war. That kind of changed everything. From Detroit, my father went to an engineering job in Reading, Pennsylvania. The owners of the copper companies viewed my father as a villain because of the new techniques he brought in, and he was eventually out of a job. So, he went to work for the government during the war years."

Fortunately, the local school Mulligan attended in Reading had a good band and a good bandmaster who played interesting music. Mulligan won first solo chair for clarinet and was able to study with the owner of a local music store, Sam Correnti, who persuaded him to try arranging. "He introduced me to all kinds of things, like jazz solos off of records. And the high school bandmaster used to take me with him on some of his professional dates as a first clarinetist. He used to like it when I would improvise on the solo parts." One of Mulligan's high school bandmates was Dick Hafer, who later played tenor saxophone in bands led by Charlie Barnet, Woody Herman, and Jimmy Dorsey. In an interview with Mark Myers of the blog JazzWax, Hafer recalled that Mulligan "knew all the hip tunes that were on the radio and could arrange them by ear in a flash. He was a great guy, a born genius."

Asked by Michael Bourne, in the January 1989 issue of *Down Beat*, when he'd known he'd become a musician, Mulligan replied: "It was conditioned in me from childhood to have a band, to write for bands, to play with bands. I have a feeling that no matter what era I lived in, a hundred years ago or a hundred years from now, I'd always be interested in orchestration. It's one of those things that's a mystery to anybody who doesn't have an ear or talent for orchestration: why does some kid come along and know how it's done? And when I was a kid, I knew how it was done, and I wanted to do it. I really wanted to go to music school and study composition, but I never got the chance."

Mulligan had started a quartet with other kids in the school in Reading and met a piano player who had played with Johnny Warrington in Philadelphia. "So, when the family was getting ready to move to Philadelphia, he suggested I go to see Johnny Warrington."

2

'A BAND TOTALLY UNLIKE OTHERS I HAD WRITTEN FOR'

Mulligan's first professional job was with bandleader Tommy Tucker, who hired him as an arranger and took him out on the road for three months. Tucker, who played piano, trumpet, and trombone, was a popular bandleader mostly associated with "sweet" music. His biggest hit was "I Don't Want to Set the World on Fire," recorded in 1941.

The job with Tucker ended after the initial three months because Mulligan's arrangements were too jazz-oriented for Tucker's taste. Mulligan returned to Philadelphia and began working as an arranger for Elliot Lawrence, who had succeeded Johnny Warrington as leader of the WCAU band. Lawrence and Mulligan had become good friends in the early '40s. "Gerry did not get along with his own family," Lawrence told me. "He hung around with me, and sometimes he would bunk down with my parents outside of Philadelphia. We were very close. He wanted to be a jazz tenor player, but he was sixteen or seventeen and the older musicians would make fun of him. Gerry started to write for my band even before I took over as musical director of WCAU. He and [trumpeter] Red Rodney were into the early days of bebop. They got me into listening to it, and that's how Gerry started to write for the band. Gerry was given the jazz things—the 'hot' things—and I wrote the ballads. He wrote the first arrangements for 'How High the Moon,' 'Just You, Just Me,' and 'Jeepers Creepers.'" Mulligan remembered that he and Lawrence "spent a lot of time together, and this created some resentment with musicians in the band."

During World War II, late-night broadcasts from clubs were shut down, but people could hear bands on the radio. "They heard our band," Lawrence said. "We got those spots." It didn't hurt that Lawrence's father was the program director. "That," said Lawrence, "was the start of my long relationship with Gerry."

The relationship took a hit when drummer Gene Krupa came into the Earle theater in Philadelphia in 1946 and hired Mulligan and Rodney away from Lawrence. "They gave me less than two weeks' notice," Lawrence said, "because Krupa was going to leave Philadelphia. They went with him, and that was the end of my first Gerry Mulligan era."

Lawrence was eventually signed to a recording contract by Columbia Records and continued to incorporate Mulligan arrangements into his repertoire. "Gerry wrote from wherever he was on the road. I bought a lot of his arrangements—'Between the Devil and the Deep Blue Sea,' 'Swingin' Door,' 'Happy Hooligan.' When I reorganized the band on the road, he came back and played baritone with the band. I don't remember the year, but it was before he went to California in the early '50s."

In February 1946, Mulligan moved to New York to join Krupa's band, where he was given an opportunity to perform, playing alto and tenor saxophone. His first arrangement to be recorded was "Disc Jockey Jump," which became a hit. Krupa described it to George T. Simon, for Simon's book *The Big Bands*, as "good both musically and commercially," adding that Mulligan "was sort of a temperamental kid who always wanted to expound on a lot of his musical ideas." Mulligan recalled how he first got recruited to play in the band's saxophone section: "Somebody got sick, so one time I got pressed into service when we were doing a split week in theaters in Ohio and Indiana. I was playing second alto. Harry Farrell was the lead alto man. He was kind of a sergeant at arms of the band. I was the arranger for the band, and I was impatient sometimes playing four or five shows a day, playing these ballad things, some of which I wrote. I was always changing notes, and this used to drive Harry crazy. In one show in Akron, Ohio, he got so mad at me that when the curtain had just come down, he turned around, put his horn down, and lunged for me."

After Krupa intervened, Mulligan promised Farrell to play the notes and not mess around with them. "I was a terrible sideman," Mulligan admitted, "because I didn't know what my own boundaries were, and I was always stepping on people's toes. One time, after a particularly hard trip, we were all kind of exhausted when we played a job, and the band really sounded sloppy. I got up out of my seat and turned around and said, 'The band sounds so sloppy. What's the matter with you guys?' Gene was looking at me in kind of stunned surprise. 'I'm sorry, old man,' he said, 'but your outburst is unforgivable.' So that was the end of my playing career with the band. But I kept on writing for them after that."

In an interview with *Cadence*'s Bob Rusch, Mulligan recalled his irregular playing opportunities with Tucker, Lawrence, and Krupa. "I never played with any of those bands unless someone got sick," he said. "I played with Elliot's band on tenor for a while because the tenor player fell on the stairs, on his children's roller skates, and broke his wrist. In Krupa's band, I wound up playing alto for a while because a guy got sick. So I was primarily an arranger and not concerned with playing with bands."

Mulligan did gain some confidence as a player while still part of Lawrence's band, as a result of an encounter with Charlie Parker. "I went to a session one time after I met him," he recalled in *Listen: Gerry Mulligan.* "He told me to come to the session and bring my horn. I said I'd be embarrassed to death to bring my horn to a session with the likes of him and [tenor saxophonist] Don Byas and Dizzy Gillespie. He said, 'No, no, bring it anyway.' So I did. I managed to hide the horn out of the way and listened for the rest of the evening. It was getting late, so I said, 'Charlie, thanks a lot. I'm leaving now, just wanted to say good-bye.' He said, 'No, wait a minute.' He went to where my horn was and took it up on the stand, and said, 'Here, play.' Imagine a seventeen-year-old kid getting on a bandstand with Charlie Parker and Don Byas. It takes the kind of guts you can only have when you're seventeen. Well, I played; I had to. He told me he liked the way I sounded and that I should play more. So, I did."

Mulligan credited Krupa for exposing him to the classical composers. "The person who really got me started listening to specific composers and trying to understand what they were doing was Gene Krupa," he said. "Gene used to carry a phonograph and records on the road, and he used to enjoy having some of the musicians hang out with him in his hotel room, where he'd play stuff for us. He had such enthusiasm for the music. He'd say, 'Now listen to this, and listen to what the trumpets do here, and listen to the timps here.' He'd focus us in on things, and it really had a good effect. The best way to learn about something new is to have somebody who's enthusiastic and who zeroes in on aspects of the music that you might miss if left to your own devices."

During his time with Krupa, Mulligan first became interested in the baritone saxophone. "I was really fascinated with the role the baritone played in the band," he said. "It wasn't just the bottom-note instrument. A lot of the arrangers I liked used it in a way that was very melodic. And Ellington wrote the top line—the melody line—for the trumpet, and he wrote a bottom line that was for the baritone. And there was a lot of contrary motion in these two lines. That means the baritone line was essential to the ensemble. I liked that very much. And there were other bands around that featured the baritone.

"For instance, Ozzie Nelson had a very good band which tried to develop its own recognizable sound. The sound in the Ozzie Nelson band was an ensemble that was pretty straight-ahead writing, but with baritone sax obbligatos wandering through it. He used this device a lot, and it really worked. I think that, as much as anything, led me to the possibilities of the baritone. Most of the bands, when they added a fifth sax, a baritone, they stuck it on the bottom like a tuba, boring to play. But if you got something interesting in the ensemble—a great register, like a cello in an orchestra—it was a beautiful register in relation to the whole ensemble. When people ask me, 'Why did you choose baritone instead of alto?' I say, 'Well, if I had been a string player in my youth, I probably would have chosen cello over violin.'"

Mulligan sold all of his horns except the baritone, telling *Cadence*'s Rusch that he, "loved the sound of Harry Carney with Duke's band and was very influenced by that." He also admired a baritone player in Nelson's band by the name of Skip Martin, "who also wrote a lot of the charts. So it's things like that that wound up creating an interest in me."

In 1958, Krupa recorded *Gene Krupa Plays Gerry Mulligan Arrangements* on the Verve label. The album, which included "Disc Jockey Jump," featured Danny Bank on baritone saxophone. According to Ken Dryden's review on the website AllMusic, "Danny Bank is a bit disappointing compared to what Mulligan could have recorded on the instrument, though it would have been unlikely that the composer would have been interested in rejoining Krupa, even for one record date, at the time it was recorded."

Mulligan stayed with Krupa for about a year as an arranger and then joined Claude Thornhill's band as an arranger, sometimes playing saxophone. Thornhill's band also included Gil Evans—an arranger who later collaborated with Mulligan, Miles Davis, and John Lewis on the groundbreaking *Birth of the Cool* recording. In the liner notes to Thornhill's *Best of Big Bands* collection, Mulligan told writer Will Friedwald that the Thornhill band had "a sense of the mystical . . . and all that came from Claude. The idea of the whole ambience of the sound, the kind of voicings that were more orchestral than band-like, that was all Claude's doing . . . It gave me the opportunity to write for a band that was totally unlike the others that I had written for." Mulligan never intended to play with the Thornhill band, but "we were going out on a tour, and Gil and Claude both wanted me to go with the band." Mulligan had been playing in impromptu sessions with the band's rhythm section and clarinetist Danny Polo, "so it seemed a natural evolution to go out and play with the band for a while. It was a good period for me. Being with Danny was kind of a settling experience because Danny was very mature, gentle, and kind of spiritual."

The move to Thornhill, according to Jerome Klinkowitz in *Listen: Gerry Mulligan—An Aural Narrative in Jazz,* "[signaled] Mulligan's transition from the characteristically prewar world of big-band jazz to the emergence of bebop and smaller group ensembles . . . Thornhill's choice for instrumentation exploded the customary form of four or five saxes and three trumpets and trombones by featuring as many as seven reed players—two on clarinet at all times, and four or five on saxes, making it possible through doubling to present a choir of seven clarinets on occasion. There are also two French horns, and occasionally a single trombone or tuba would be scored to play above the trumpets rather than below them . . . Suddenly, Claude Thornhill and his orchestra became the focal point for serious, forward-looking musicians."

Mulligan had actually been a big fan of the Thornhill band when he was in high school. "I started getting Thornhill records," he said. "The sound of the band was beautiful. I always thought that Claude approached writing for the band from the bandstand as if it were an orchestra, even though there were no strings. In his early bands, it was five brass, four saxes, plus two clarinets. He managed to get those orchestral sounds that way. It was the clarinets that did it." Mulligan recalled that in 1939, Glenn Miller had a daily half-hour broadcast followed by another thirty minutes featuring Thornhill's band. "When Miller and his band were drafted into the service, Claude was given the Glenn Miller time spot. So he was really set up to become the most popular band in the country. Then Claude got drafted." While Miller received lots of publicity as an Air Force colonel, Thornhill was a Navy chief petty officer and ended up being sent to the South Pacific as the piano player in Artie Shaw's band. "By all accounts," Mulligan said, "I heard that Claude was remarkable out there. He would try to make good music for the guys as they island-hopped."

On May 8, 2009, Kevin Blancq, a trumpeter who directs the jazz bands at the LaGuardia High School of Music & Art in New York City, presented a concert in tribute to Thornhill at the Thalia theater on New York's Upper West Side. Writing about the concert, Friedwald said that Thornhill "and his amazing staff of orchestrators and soloists . . . saw the future and boldly went where no musicians had gone before. The band, which made its mark throughout the high years of the swing era and the early postwar period, cast an enormous influence on the shape of the jazz to come." Friedwald added that when *Birth of the Cool* was introduced, "most of the musicians involved" were longtime Thornhill admirers: Gil Evans, Lee Konitz, and Gerry Mulligan.

In 1961, Mulligan told the *New York Herald Tribune*'s George T. Simon that he "learned the art of underblowing, or controlled violence, and still getting a full, rich sound, from working in Claude Thornhill's band." Mulligan, Simon wrote, "feels this [the Thornhill band] was easily the most underrated big band of all time."

While working in the Thornhill band, Mulligan began spending time with Evans at Evans's West 55th Street apartment in New York. That's when the arrangements Mulligan and Evans wrote for Thornhill began to shape the eventual creation of the *Birth of the Cool* band. Among the Mulligan arrangements that Thornhill featured in the late '40s were "Elevation," "Godchild," and "Sometimes I'm Happy." The British writer and arranger Brian Priestly described the Evans/Mulligan arrangements for Thornhill as "jazz-oriented instrumentals" that "swung without shouting, and hinted at a bebop equivalent of early Count Basie and Lester Young."

3

'OUT OF THE BASEMENT AND . . . INTO A REHEARSAL HALL'

When he recalled what was developing in Evans's apartment, Mulligan described "a kind of exaggerated bohemian attitude. We were living in the middle of Fifth Avenue and 55th Street. Miles [Davis] and I would walk down the street, and people would stare at us. Miles would really get mad, and I'd say, 'You got to admit we're really a strange-looking pair, walking around here.'" During this time, Mulligan was "messing around with heroin, but I hadn't gotten myself totally strung out yet. Every time I see a photograph of myself during this period, I never see a photograph of myself smiling. I guess music was my one joy; the rest of it was very difficult."

The inside of the West 55th Street apartment was described by composer George Russell to Nat Hentoff in *Jazz Is*. "A very big bed took up a lot of the place," Russell said. "There was one big lamp and a cat named Becky. The linoleum was battered, and there was a little court outside. Inside, it was always very dark. The feeling of the room was timelessness. Whenever you went there, you wouldn't care about conditions outside. You couldn't tell whether it was day or night, summer or winter, and it didn't matter. At all hours, the place was loaded with people who came in and out."

Mulligan actually had his own furnished room in somebody else's apartment near Madison Square Garden, but he didn't spend much time there. "I was over at Gil's place most of the time," he said. "It finally got to the point where Gil and I were taking turns using the piano and taking turns sleeping. And there were people in and out of the place all the time. This went on in winter and summer. When it got really cold, we were bundled up in overcoats, sitting at the piano, writing. There were open-minded conversations always going on—George Russell, John Lewis, occasionally Johnny Mandel, [pianist and songwriter] John Benson Brooks, [trumpeter Johnny] Carisi, the guys from Thornhill's band, when they were in town, [vocalist] Dave Lambert. All of us felt like a transient existence."

At the time, according to Frank Tirro in his *The Birth of the Cool of Miles Davis and His Associates*, "Mulligan was circulating among the best of the swing and modern musicians, including Charlie Parker. Both his performing talent and his precocious genius were clearly recognized by his colleagues.

"Mulligan, like Evans, gained his compositional skills and arranging craft, not at a college or conservatory, but on his own . . . While performing and arranging for the Claude Thornhill Orchestra, he [Mulligan] played clarinet as well as tenor and baritone saxophones, and it was after their meeting in this band that he and Evans began planning a small ensemble with Thornhill sound capabilities."

Musically, Mulligan and Evans began thinking about how to put a band together, whether it should be a small band or a big band. One thing they agreed on, Mulligan said, was that "it had to be something that would give the possibilities to the writers and try to combine that with a setting that would allow the horn players to sound their best."

When the writing began, Mulligan said, "Davis was really the practical one. Miles always wanted something of his own. He really had a desire to have his own band and make a place for himself in the music scene. He loved the sound of the Thornhill band. When he heard this idea we were talking about with the instrumentation, he thought that could be it. So he was the one who started making the phone calls and getting the players together and reserving the rehearsal studios and generally assuming the role of the leader. And that's how we really started playing. If it had been left to the rest of us, we'd have kept on theorizing and writing and never getting around to doing anything. The idea of that band started off as a rehearsal band. We started off to play the stuff—we really didn't know what we were doing. Miles had a more definite idea of what he wanted to do, which I don't think Gil Evans or John Lewis or I thought about particularly. We had dreamed up this instrumentation. We just wanted to try it.

"We finally wound up with six horns because it seemed to offer a lot of possibilities. Originally, we thought we'd have Danny Polo on clarinet, but we realized that was impractical because Danny was always on the road with the Thornhill band, and there wasn't anybody else we wanted on clarinet. We wound up holding it to one trumpet because if Miles was going to be the trumpet, his sound was so personal; we didn't want to blend it with another trumpet sound.

"We tried to have enough low horns to be able to use the tuba. In some ways, the tuba was like a string instrument, especially when you realize the amplified bass gives the bass another presence in the band, and the tuba lines get in the way of the bass lines and vice versa. We wanted the tuba because we wanted a chromatic scale to the band. Not having a clarinet or flute kind of restricted us at the top. The overall ensemble of those six horns playing together had a unique sound and a good ensemble sound. We got two high voices, two middle voices, and two low voices, so they could be used in very different ways, contrapuntally or breaking up into several different small ensembles. So, it did indeed offer the possibilities we were looking for, giving the most latitude for the writer, the most freedom and the best setting for the soloist. That was the basis of it and the result of a lot of theorizing."

The Capitol Records *Birth of the Cool* album was actually recorded in three different sessions. Four of the six horns were the same on all three sessions: Davis on trumpet, Bill Barber on tuba, Lee Konitz on alto sax, and Mulligan on baritone sax. J. J. Johnson played trombone on two sessions; Kai Winding on the other. There were three different French horn players: Junior Collins, Sandy Siegelstein, and Gunther Schuller. As for the rhythm section, Max Roach and Kenny Clarke were the drummers; Al Haig and John Lewis alternated on piano; and three different bassists participated: Joe Shulman, Nelson Boyd, and Al McKibbon. The one vocal, "Darn That Dream," was sung by Kenny Hagood.

In a 1992 interview with the *Chicago Tribune*'s Howard Reich, Mulligan said that "Miles wanted Sonny Stitt [as the alto saxophonist]," but "Gil and I both wanted Lee Konitz. His playing with Claude Thornhill's band sounded so wonderful that we thought he would be the perfect foil opposite Miles . . . Lee had that liquid tone that fit into our concept of the ensemble so well."

Bill Charlap, a pianist who played with Mulligan's quartet in the 1980s, told me Davis was "the charismatic catalyst. Miles's improvisations were lyrical and profound. All of those solos on *Birth of the Cool* were perfect, but not perfect with a bow on them. You still hear him stretching. You still hear him, maybe missing, but making it right on the next thing he plays. It's the feeling of jazz really being extemporaneous."

Gunther Schuller, then a French horn player in the Metropolitan Opera Orchestra, recalled being recruited by Davis, in his book *A Life in Pursuit of Music and Beauty*: "Miles actually came to the Met to meet with me, to personally check me out, since he had never heard me play, and to go over the horn parts with me. I have to think that Miles may have been the first jazz or black musician to ever set foot in the musicians' locker room in the then lily-white, 67-year-old Metropolitan Opera House."

The mixed-race aspect of the recording that eventually took place was, in fact, groundbreaking. This was pointed out by Stanley Crouch in his chapter on Davis in *Considering Genius*. "The whole effort," he wrote, "symbolized an interracial cooperation that had no real precedent in jazz history. White musicians had been influenced by many black musicians, and Negroes had been influenced by a few white musicians; they had all jammed together on hundreds upon hundreds of nights; beginning with Benny Goodman's Quartet, featuring Lionel Hampton and Teddy Wilson, they had started working together in public; but close collaboration of the sort Davis and John Lewis had with Gerry Mulligan, Gil Evans, and Johnny Carisi had not happened before."

Miles, Mulligan said, took the project "out of the basement and put it into a rehearsal hall, but that was kind of a mixed blessing. When we got to work, Miles didn't have the ability to take over as a leader. As a consequence, there would be friction about interpretation or who's soloing or whatever; and Miles would just let the thing play. And things would fester and you would have some sort of warfare. It happens when you put talented people together. You have to have a leader who will lay down the law. A band is no place for a democracy. Miles was the leader and provided the sound of the band, but John Lewis and I did the bulk of the writing."

In fact, Mulligan arranged six of the album's twelve selections: George

Wallington's "Godchild," Davis's "Deception," the Eddie De Lange/Jimmy Van Heusen song "Darn That Dream," and three of his own original compositions: "Jeru," "Rocker," and "Venus de Milo." Lewis arranged the Davis/Bud Powell composition "Budo," Denzil Best's "Move," and his own "Rouge." Evans arranged "Boplicity," which he cowrote with Davis (it was credited to Davis's mother, Cleo Henry, because the trumpeter wanted the song handled by a different publishing house), and "Moon Dreams," written by Chummy MacGregor and Johnny Mercer. Trumpeter Johnny Carisi arranged his own composition, "Israel." Mulligan also composed and arranged "Joost at the Roost," a tune played by the band but not included on the album.

Despite the fact that half of the recorded selections were arranged by Mulligan and three were written by him, he never really received the recognition he deserved. In his doctoral dissertation at the University of Maryland, Richard Samuel Fine pointed out that "with each subsequent release of *Birth of the Cool* albums, the 'classic' stature of the nonet continues to rise with most of the credit going to Davis and Evans, leaving Gerry Mulligan somewhat shortchanged from an appreciation standpoint. Mulligan's contribution has been minimized by the jazz press, even though his role was central. He was the only participant to continue working with the nonet's music with, for example, his recordings of 'Rocker' and 'Godchild' by his early '50s tentette, and his recording of 'Israel' by his '60s concert jazz band." John McNeil, a trumpeter who played with Mulligan's concert jazz band in the '70s, echoed Fine. "Most of the credit for *Birth of the Cool*," McNeil told me, "went to Gil Evans. Equal credit should have been given to Gerry Mulligan."

Frank Tirro says that "Jeru" "is a jazz masterpiece, and, in its economy, it is truly a work of compositional genius. Its arrangement is masterful as well . . . and its performance, too, stands at the pinnacle of the numbers recorded by the nonet in the studio. 'Jeru' has become a jazz standard, and, over the years, it has shown its adaptability by receiving successful treatments from solo piano renditions to big-band orchestrations." "Jeru" also became Mulligan's nickname, reportedly given to him by Davis.

In a review that appears on AllMusic, Stephen Thomas Erlewine mistakenly gave credit to Evans for all of the arrangements, a misconception that is apparently shared by others as well. Art Farmer, the late trumpeter/

flugelhornist who played with Mulligan in the late '50s, sought to put this inaccuracy to rest in *Listen: Gerry Mulligan.* "When you think of *Birth of the Cool*," he said, "Gil Evans gets most of the credit for that, but Gerry did most of the arranging. It wasn't Gil. I don't know if Gerry will ever be recognized for that."

Jon Newsom, retired chief of the Music Division at the Library of Congress, who established the Gerry Mulligan Collection there in the 1990s, acknowledged that "Miles Davis was brilliant, and Gil Evans went on and did absolutely fantastic things. But those classic recordings," he told me, "are more Gerry than anybody else."

Ian Kendall, writing in *Jazz Journal International*, lamented "a tendency to play down Mulligan's role in the innovations of the Miles Davis Nonet recordings of 1948 to 1950." Richard Cook, in *Jazz Review*, pointed out that "Simple guides to jazz tend to signpost the *Birth of the Cool* as a Miles Davis–Gil Evans project. But Gerry Mulligan . . . casts a long shadow over the sound of this prototypical 'modern' ensemble: not just through his lean, sonorous baritone parts, but in the timbres of brass and woodwinds which predominate as the insignia of cool. You can hear just the same sort of thing—with a steadily evolving artistry—in every Mulligan chart set down in the '50s." And the *Chicago Tribune*'s Reich added, "Were it not for Mulligan, the obscure, 1949–50 recordings that years later would be relaunched as Miles Davis's seminal *Birth of the Cool* album might never have attained their particular melodic luster."

Pianist Roger Kellaway, who played on Mulligan's groundbreaking album *The Age of Steam* in the early 1970s, thinks *Birth of the Cool* is "a project that stands up to this day because you can listen to it and hear things that you may never have heard, even in all this time." Speaking in a video interview packaged as part of the *Listen: Gerry Mulligan* documentary, Kellaway emphasized that *Birth of the Cool* had "so much imagination, everything is so cohesive. It became kind of a chamber ensemble. I didn't know until years later that Gerry did a lot of those charts. I can't really talk specifically about Gerry's arranging ability, other than the thing that always interests me about his charts is imagination and how the sound spectrum is handled. You could certainly draw a relationship between *Birth of the Cool* and Gerry Mulligan and Chet Baker or Gerry Mulligan and Bob Brookmeyer (collaborations that would come later). Gerry had a beautiful way of handling silence, very simple lines. That was very impressive to me, being an accompanist."

Davis secured the recording contract with Capitol, which, according to Mulligan, was "one of the two or three times Capitol Records discovered jazz. They wound up signing various of us to different kinds of contracts." The band had a multiweek engagement at New York's Royal Roost, but Mulligan didn't believe the band had really come together. "We really needed more concentration on how to do it. If you start stretching out too many solos on those arrangements, if the solos are too long, then the composed parts lose their continuity. That's what Miles started to do in the club, so the band never really solved those problems. John Lewis used to really get upset with him. There were lots of divisive things going on instead of the band being focused in on itself, discussing the musical problems and working on them."

The recording sessions, Mulligan said, "were different because you were not dealing with an audience. You're dealing with the music, your part in the music and in the ensemble. Capitol sent Pete Rugolo (lead arranger/composer for the Stan Kenton Orchestra) in from Los Angeles to supervise, and Pete hadn't been around the band. He had a terrible time in the control room. I told him all we were trying to do was get a natural balance among the six horns, which was already a challenge because the volume range of these six horns was so varied. To be able to balance the volume of the tuba, for instance, with volume of the trumpet or alto is something that we've got to consider all the time. What we did have was the overall quality and atmosphere of the band, and it had the melodic sense of all the things that were going on. With all of the musical imperfections, the musical perfection was there. Miles was brilliant. That made everything worthwhile. The other thing that made it worthwhile was Max Roach on the first set of dates. He was wonderful. He was far and away the best drummer for this. He approached it as a composer and took the kind of care playing with the ensemble that gave compositional awareness. I loved the way he played."

Schuller recalled that he got to his recording date a half hour early. "I was really anxious," he wrote, "not only because it was my most important involvement with jazz to date—a virtual nobody, suddenly working with some of the finest jazz talents in the world—but also because, as a very experienced musician in classical preparation procedures, I worried how we would be able to record so much new and difficult music in a three-hour record session. So were J. J. [Johnson] and Bill Barber. We were especially worried about how we were going to get through the coda in 'Moon Dreams.'"

The band did not stay together very long after the Royal Roost engagements, and the recording was not a success. New Jersey City University jazz studies professor Dick Lowenthal recalled to me a conversation with Mulligan about the *Birth of the Cool* experience when Lowenthal hired him in the '70s to talk to students in a jazz history course. "He said that when they recorded it, Capitol Records really thought they were going to have a popular album on their hands. That's what it was going to be marketed as. That album got buried for about nine or ten years. And then, when it was reissued later, everyone said, 'Ooh, listen to how new that sounds.'"

The legacy of the recording was enormous. Composer-conductor-multi-instrumentalist David Amram, in *Listen: Gerry Mulligan*, called *Birth of the Cool* "remarkable. It was something that was magnificent and still endures all these years later." A 2009 article on the *Guardian*'s website acknowledged that the recording was "a commercial disaster," but that it "illuminated a new bebop language, one that would pave the way for jazz in the 1950s and lay the foundations for Davis's seminal *Kind of Blue*."

Erlewine said that *Birth of the Cool* "remains one of the defining, pivotal moments in jazz. This is where the elasticity of bop was married with skillful big-band arrangements and a relaxed, subdued mood that made it all seem easy even at its most intricate. After all, there's a reason why this music was called cool; it has a hip, detached elegance, never getting too hot, even as the rhythms skip and jump . . . this music is so inventive, it remains alluring even after its influence has been thoroughly absorbed into the mainstream."

Since the project involved so many writers, Mark Gardner, writing in *The Blackwell Guide to Recorded Jazz*, said, "the oneness of feeling they achieved is a tribute to their unity of purpose." Gardner added that many of the principal players and writers went on to expand on the "cool" concept—"Davis in his own groups and through the later orchestral collaborations with Evans, Lewis through the Modern Jazz Quartet, Mulligan in his quartet, tentette, and concert jazz band, Konitz within a series of combos and elaborations with [pianist] Lennie Tristano." What the band ultimately accomplished, according to Gardner, "was the existence of new avenues and possibilities for modern jazz." The band, he said, even had an impact on "bop's hottest soloist, Charlie Parker, who, a few months after Davis's recording was released, commissioned Mulligan to arrange 'Rocker' for a string ensemble that the alto saxophonist was fronting. 'Rocker' became a fixture in Parker's book with the stiff string section, and he would even play the composition with his quintet."

Jazz historian Bill Kirchner believes the influence of *Birth of the Cool* can be "compared to the Louis Armstrong Hot Fives and Sevens and to other classics by Duke Ellington, Count Basie, and Charlie Parker. These recordings had an enormous influence on musicians and the jazz public," he said in a *Jazz Journal* article by Gordon Jack.

4

'HE WOULD PLAY FANTASTICALLY'

While the Krupa-Thornhill-Davis era was an incredibly creative period for Mulligan, what is remarkable is that his accomplishments occurred while he was addicted to heroin. "Writing was taking more and more out of me," he recalled. "The days I was using drugs, there was less time to focus on music. When I was using heroin, I would forget about everything for twelve to eighteen hours at a stretch."

After the *Birth of the Cool* experience, Mulligan found himself broke and decided to hitchhike west with his girlfriend, Gail Madden. Bassist Bill Crow remembers meeting Madden while the couple was still in New York. "I got called for a job out in Long Island City," he recalled. "It was a low-paying job, but they needed a bass player. One of the attractions was that Gerry was going to be there. Gail was there and obviously was with Gerry. She was not only there, but she was playing maracas with the band. Her idea was to get all these talented people like Bird, Sonny Stitt, Gerry—guys that were strung out a little bit—get them off junk, get their heads straightened out, and get them to be more productive." According to writer Martin Abramson (in James Gavin's book *Deep in a Dream: The Long Night of Chet Baker*), Madden believed "she could help addicts with the power of suggestion."

Crow recalled another session that took place between *Birth of the Cool* and Mulligan's departure for the West Coast. "I had heard that Gerry was going to have a rehearsal with some of his big-band charts for anyone that wanted to come and play them. It was a Monday afternoon, and I decided to go and hear some music. No one could afford the studio, so Gerry said, 'It's a nice day. Why don't we go out in Central Park?' So he set up just south of 72nd Street. He didn't have a drummer. He had two bass players, four trumpets, five saxes, and him and Gail. Everybody was just sitting on the ground looking at their parts. It sounded great—Brew Moore (tenor sax), Nick Travis (trumpet), Allan Eager (alto, tenor), Phil Leshin (bass). The following week, a couple of the junkies in the band said, 'Why don't we set up near the men's room where we can shoot up?' Of course the men's room attendant called the cops, and, since they didn't have a permit to play in the park, the cop made them go away.

"I heard that Gerry and Gail had set out hitchhiking for Los Angeles," Crow continued, "and, by God, they made it. Gerry wasn't a big junkie; no one could afford to be. Well, she got him off the junk on the way out there, and he got established in California."

Prior to leaving for California, Mulligan was also briefly reunited with Elliot Lawrence. "I was reorganizing my band on the road," Lawrence remembered. "Gerry came and played baritone with my band. I don't recall exactly the year, but it was before he went to California. He was on drugs, as was most of my band. He made my life miserable." Lawrence recalled one occurrence in Virginia when the band was booked to play at a women's college—"one of those fancy women's finishing schools. They put the band up in the main building, an old Southern mansion. At 3 a.m., Gerry and a couple of the other guys were out of drugs and started screaming. I can still see the housemothers in their curlers. We tried to bang on Gerry's door, and they had put furniture up against the door. We couldn't open the door, and the school had to call the fire department." Despite incidents such as this, Lawrence put up with it because, "all this time, [Gerry] would play fantastically, as he always did."

Upon arriving in Los Angeles, Mulligan was able to make a connection with Stan Kenton through an arranger named Bob Graettinger, a former boyfriend of Madden's. "I had an opportunity to write for the [Kenton] band," Mulligan recalled, "and, even though it wasn't my ideal band, I was very glad to have the job to write for them, and I did my best to satisfy the leader. So I wrote a lot of charts. The first thing I wrote was very contrapuntal. I was trying to do a thing that built an ensemble sound out of unison contrapuntal lines. And it built up to a nice, solid ensemble for us. Stan didn't really like it very well, so I had to rewrite it. He put the tune 'Walkin' Shoes' on the first part and used the out chorus from the piece that was there. I was always amused by the fact that Stan had gotten stuck with me. He had been doing all these experimental things, and this time he was going to have a band for musicians. This was going to be his swing band. Because the musicians liked my charts, he felt he had to buy them."

Writing about the two men's relationship in the May 26, 1960, issue of *Down Beat*, Leonard Feather confirmed Kenton's band members' enthusiasm for Mulligan's music: "Though the music he wrote (ten charts in all) was not quite startlingly colorful enough to elicit the unbounded enthusiasm of Kenton himself, many musicians both in and out of the band felt that the Mulligan contributions were among the swinging-est pieces ever inserted in the Kenton books. Some of them were used only as throwaways on dance dates. But Kenton did record two of Mulligan's originals, 'Swing House' and 'Young Blood,' and continued to play the latter frequently long after Mulligan stopped writing for the band."

The Kenton work was Mulligan's main source of income, but "I started playing around town, too," Mulligan said. "When the Kenton band went on the road, I had to find other things to do. One of the few people in California who was helpful to me at that point was [trumpeter] Shorty Rogers. He tried to get me on record dates and gigs, and I wound up down at the Lighthouse in Hermosa Beach. It was probably about this time that Gail and I split up. That left me by myself in L.A. I spent a lot of time going to sessions and trying to find jobs. At the Lighthouse, I would start at 3 p.m. on Saturday and play until three in the morning. Then we were back there at three o'clock on Sunday afternoon until three o'clock Monday morning. I did that for quite a number of months, and then one weekend it really got to me."

Around this time, Mulligan met Dick Bock, a record producer for Discovery Records who was also booking music for the Haig, a small jazz club in the Wilshire section of Los Angeles. Bock hired Mulligan to lead a group on the off night, opposite Erroll Garner. "They had a beautiful piano in the place for Erroll," Mulligan explained to me when I interviewed him in 1981. "When Erroll was finished with his engagement, they were bringing in Red Norvo's trio, which consisted of Red on vibes, Red Mitchell on bass, and Tal Farlow on guitar. No piano.

"They weren't going to have a piano in the club. They said that, for the off night, they would get a little spinet or something that didn't take up much room and wasn't expensive. I said, 'Forget it. I'll put a group together without a piano,' and we won't have to bother with it at all." The quartet (Chet Baker on trumpet, Chico Hamilton on drums, and Bob Whitlock on bass) was an instant success, playing what Mulligan described as "improvised counterpoint—having the two horns operate over the bass line."

5

'THAT RARE KIND OF JAZZ WHICH APPEALS TO EVERYONE'

Mulligan hired Bob Whitlock as his bassist first, and Whitlock recommended Chet Baker, who had played at some jam sessions in the San Fernando Valley with Mulligan. "I was very impressed with his melodic playing," Mulligan said. "You don't usually hear that in players from jam sessions. People are usually so busy working on their techniques. Chet was such a melodic player that I thought I could try it with no piano. Chet and I could do things where we'd play tunes we hadn't even discussed. We'd wind up doing something that sounded like an organized arrangement. It was one of the joys of playing with Chet—a musical compatibility I had never experienced before."

In *Deep in a Dream*, Gavin underscored this compatibility: Mulligan, he wrote, "loved melody as much as he [Baker] did" and "saw a solo as a work of architecture, not as an excuse to blow. Most horn-playing duos took turns soloing, then competitively traded 'fours' and 'eights' (four-and eight-bar phrases), but Baker and Mulligan each checked their egos and looked for ways to complement each other. They played in unison or harmony, broke into effortless counterpoint."

Mark Gardner pointed out that "Baker flourished among the popular songs and catchy originals worked up by Mulligan. Neither musician was hampered by the absence of keyboard feeds, although each would often provide helpful riffs when the other was improvising. A natural outcome of this procedure was that an abundance of contrapuntal interweaving between saxophone and trumpet became one of the distinctive features of the group's recordings. The musical understanding within this partnership was remarkably loose, each man seemingly able to anticipate the next thought of the other. Their personal relationship was less harmonious, yet these discords were buried when it was time to play."

Chico Hamilton had been playing with Charlie Barnet's band at a club called Streets of Paris on Hollywood Boulevard. Chico, Mulligan said, "had his own unique approach. All the time we rehearsed, he rehearsed with a small set—a snare drum and a hi-hat and a tom-tom, a minimal set. We were rehearsing in a house that Chet had rented in Watts, and he wanted to bring his whole set to the gig, but I convinced him to just bring what we had been rehearsing with. Chico had such a good show sense that he brought that out in all of us. So, as introverted as Chet and I were, there was a quality about the music that wasn't. What we were doing was very accessible, and Chico brought this kind of extroverted quality to it that kind of kept the thing alive. I fell into a natural role of accompanying, being the bridge between the bass line and the solo line; and it worked."

Mulligan remembered the Haig experience as "a phenomenal thing. We found ourselves with lines outside, people waiting to get in. And it happened so quickly that I was really unprepared for it. We played on the off night for as long as Red was there with his trio, about six weeks, and the audience built as we went along. So we were doing tremendous business in the place. We were all amazed. We couldn't figure it out."

About halfway into the engagement, *Time* magazine reported that "[the] hot music topic in Los Angeles last week was the cool jazz of a gaunt, hungry-looking young fellow named Gerry Mulligan who plays the baritone saxophone. For the past three months, Mulligan's quartet has been performing in a nightclub known as the Haig, a spot that has featured such stalwarts as Red Norvo and Erroll Garner—and he was drawing the biggest crowds in the club's history. Says the Haig's happy manager: 'People just like his kind of sound.'" Nat Hentoff, writing in *The New Yorker* on March 21, 1959, recalled his initial reaction to the quartet: "At first, the spontaneous counterpoint sometimes faltered, and only the bass and drums were heard, but the quartet quickly fused into an unusually flowing unit."

In a review for Amazon.co.uk of the 1991 rerelease of *The Best of the Gerry Mulligan Quartet with Chet Baker* (Pacific Jazz/Capitol), British jazz critic Dave Gelly described the impact of the pianoless quartet as "instant and far-reaching. No one had ever heard anything like it before. Baritone saxophone, trumpet, bass, and drums seemed such an unlikely combination, yet the effect was enchanting—light, supple, tuneful, witty . . . The quartet's music was that rare kind of jazz which appeals to everyone, all kinds of jazz fans and a broad section of the general public as well."

Jazz critic Gary Giddins described the pianoless quartet as "extramusical drama" in *Visions of Jazz: The First Century*. "Audiences," he wrote, "flocked to hear the dreamily supple themes and variations, but also to check out the unlikely musicians playing them. Mulligan, sporting a carrot-hued crew cut, manipulated the huge baritone as though it were an instrument renowned for wistful romance, which in his hands and no one else's it became.

"Baker, with his neatly boxed pompadour and baby-face handsomeness, was short, introverted, and intense; he was a natural, creative in any key, exceptional ears, liked to play with the mike against the bell of his trumpet, which he occasionally put aside to croon a song in a girlishly attenuated voice. That Hamilton, the curly-haired drummer with big eyes and a penchant for beating complicated rhythms with his mallets, was black added to the mystique—integrated bands were not yet the norm. Only the bassists lacked charisma. Meanwhile, the critics licked their pencils and pondered the affair of the missing piano. This was one of jazz's pointless controversies. No one called Benny Goodman's trio 'bassless' or Art Tatum's trio 'drumless.' But conventions in instrumentation had congealed by the early '50s, and the absence of a piano was considered adventurous. The Mulligan group became universally known as the 'pianoless quartet.'"

David Amram, who didn't meet or play with Mulligan until 1956, related to me the first time he heard the pianoless quartet. "I flashed back to hearing Bix Beiderbecke and then back to first hearing the Brandenburg Concertos," he said. "It was a combination of melody and counterpoint that transcended category." Alto saxophonist Phil Woods was a student at Juilliard when the pianoless quartet became popular. "All of us loved the pianoless quartet," he said. "That changed the whole world of music."

It eliminated, he told me, "the sometime tyranny of a piano player who could dictate and determine the melodic content of an improviser by his harmonic selection. I thought, 'If it was good enough for Bach, it should be good enough for bebop.'"

Dean Johnson, a bassist who played with Mulligan from 1985 until Mulligan's death in 1996, told me he believes the pianoless quartet unlocked the rhythm section and had a profound impact on the development of modern jazz. "It opened things up for the bass and drums, and Gerry was such a star in that era. The pianoless quartet put his name on the map; he was known by the regular community, not just the jazz community. If Dave Brubeck was the pinnacle, Gerry was just under that—almost on Brubeck's level."

The missing piano, in the opinion of Ted Gioia, overshadowed some of the other attributes of the quartet. "Much of the publicity surrounding the Mulligan Quartet," Gioia wrote in his book *West Coast Jazz*, "stemmed from the absence of a pianist. The jazz journals frequently referred to it as the 'pianoless quartet,' as if the group were more noteworthy for what it lacked than for what it did. Today, the omission of a harmony instrument does not sound unusual, and other virtues of this group are more salient: its effective use of counterpoint, its understated rhythm section, its melodic clarity, and its willingness to take chances. Not since the days of New Orleans ensemble playing had the individual members of a small combo been so willing to merge their personal sounds into a cohesive whole."

When the Norvo engagement ended, the quartet—minus Whitlock, who was replaced by Carson Smith—was booked into the Blackhawk in San Francisco, a gig that also attracted a recording contract. "Apparently, Dave Brubeck had been talking about the group up there," Mulligan said, "and he told Fantasy they should record us. Well, the guys from Fantasy came around, and we went up and played at the Blackhawk. That was our first steady engagement. I tended to be sympathetic to Fantasy because Dave and I had become friends. I would have loved to record for them, but I didn't think I could because I had started this thing with Dick Bock (who had started Pacific Jazz in 1952 with a recording of the Mulligan Quartet), and I felt my first commitment was to Pacific Jazz.

"But I got so much pressure from the other guys in the group because they were looking at it in terms of income. Here we were being offered an album, and it's real money, and we're turning it down. I finally knuckled under to their demands. I always felt wrong about it. The Fantasy record was on red vinyl, very high-quality stuff. That was the best album we did with the quartet. It was not really good for the relationship with Dick and Pacific Jazz, but when we went back to Los Angeles, we went back to recording with Dick. We did a lot of albums with him, and he recorded Chet with his own group."

After the Blackhawk engagement, the quartet returned to the Haig as the headliners. "Chico played with us for a while," Mulligan recalled. "Then he had a call from Lena Horne, who wanted him to come back on the road with her. He needed to make more money, so he was very apologetic about it, but he had to do it for financial reasons. I was really upset; that was the beginning of kind of a rough period. I got really angry. I was so mad, I tossed my horn across the room, stomped out of the place. That night, driving home, I was still fuming." Mulligan replaced Hamilton with Larry Bunker, a drummer who had played with saxophonists Georgie Auld and Art Pepper and pianist Hampton Hawes.

Mulligan's temper was sometimes directed toward the audience, particularly at the Haig. "It only seated ninety people, or if you really crowded them in, maybe one hundred ten," he said. "If you got one noisy table, it would make it impossible for everybody to hear. People were paying an admission to get in and were sitting there listening to the music. I would say, 'If you're looking for a place to hang out and talk, you picked the wrong room. In here, everybody is trying to listen, except you.' It was certainly unusual for a performer to tell an audience how to behave. But most of the people who came in there who made any comment about it thanked me. I spent a lot of my youth being a hard-nosed pain in the ass, but what I did at the Haig seemed perfectly justified."

(A similar scenario resurfaced more than twenty years later during an engagement of the Gerry Mulligan Quintet at Hopper's, a club in Greenwich Village. In May 1974, *Down Beat*'s Chuck Berg reported that Mulligan reacted to a "barely audible conversation" in the middle of the last set. "After having established a pleasant, 'I'm OK-You're OK' rapport with his appreciative audience," Berg wrote, "Mulligan suddenly decided his audience was *not* OK. As his slightly stunned colleagues stood by, an angry Mulligan muttered something about the offending conversation and making mistakes." According to Berg, he then "defiantly packed his horns.")

The return engagement at the Haig was originally planned for four weeks, but it was extended to more than six months. The quartet had become very popular, according to Richard Samuel Fine, because "Mulligan recognized the importance of pacing a show with a wide variety of material." Whitlock, who had returned to the quartet in 1952, when Smith went out on the road with Billy May, told Gordon Jack, author of *Fifties Jazz Talk: An Oral Retrospective*, that, "We not only played standards and originals, but also everything from Latin sambas to tunes from Disney movies. There was something for everyone, and the caliber of musicianship was always convincing."

Pointing out that "one of the highlights of a Mulligan quartet performance is the improvised weaving of contrapuntal lines of the horns and bass," Robert Gordon, writing in his book *Jazz West Coast*, added that, "The influence here is at least as much King Oliver as J. S. Bach, and the comment has often been made that the quartet was at times playing a sort of neo-Dixieland. Although this was meant as a put-down, it is an observation to which Mulligan—who has always felt respect and admiration for his jazz elders—would readily assent. Gerry knew just where his quartet stood in relation to the evolution of jazz."

"'The idea of a band without a piano is not new,' he wrote, in the liner notes introducing his first Pacific Jazz album. 'The very first jazz bands didn't use them. (How could they? They were either marching or riding in wagons.)'"

The significance of the pianoless quartet, according to Jack, was its "unique and pristine ensemble sound dominated by [Mulligan's] quite outstanding ability as an accompanist on the baritone. His skill as one of the foremost jazz writers was matched by the way he could compose instant arrangements on the bandstand, finding perfect counter lines to whatever his playing partners conceived. It was this single quality that made his groups so distinctive, for, despite becoming a virtuoso soloist, Mulligan was essentially an ensemble player, and the quartet was most definitely an ensemble—not just two soloists sharing a stage with a rhythm section."

Despite the success of the quartet, dealing with Baker had become a problem for Mulligan. The musical compatibility between the two of them did not extend to their personal relationship. "We were such totally different people, with different attitudes as to how we wanted to live. I was always kind of a loner. I had a handful of friends who I liked to hang out with, where music was the focus. Chet, on the other hand, always liked to travel with a pack of four or five guys. Chet was the leader, but it made it hard for these guys, because . . . when it came to the quartet, I was the leader."

Comparing the Mulligan-Baker musical relationship to such historic partnerships as "Joe Venuti and Eddie Lang in the 1920s, Tommy and Jimmy Dorsey in the '30s, and Dizzy Gillespie and Charlie Parker in the '40s," Leonard Feather, in the May 1960 issue of *Down Beat*, quoted Chico Hamilton as saying, "The group really came off until Gerry and Chet started hating each other. They'd come on the stand, and Gerry would face one way and Chet another. A couple of times I had to pull them apart."

During this period, Mulligan had married Jeffie Boyd, a transplanted New Yorker, who, according to Gavin, was attracted by Mulligan's brains and "leprechaunish" sense of humor. Since Gail Madden's drug cure had proved temporary, Mulligan was using again, off and on. He asked Boyd to now help him get off drugs, an effort that failed.

"Chet," Mulligan said, "liked to drive fast; he liked fast cars. During the period of time we were together, I think he went through three or four cars. They usually wound up smashed up somewhere. Chet owed so much money on cars, and he and his wife didn't have a place to stay. I let them stay temporarily in the house I was renting, and, before I knew it, the whole pack was there. They'd hang out while we were at work. Chet had this thing going on with a narcotics cop. He liked to ride Chet, and Chet liked to ride him back. I kept telling Chet to cool it—after all, you are carrying pot around, and you're a little bit vulnerable. The neighborhood sees all these guys around, playing music loud and smoking pot all over the place. So, I come home from the gig one night with Chet, and the police are there. So I got busted because it was my house." According to an account in *Deep in a Dream*, Mulligan's arrest was also due to evidence he had been taking heroin.

"I ended up being sent to the honor farm," Mulligan said, "which was part of the county jail system, for about ninety days. Chet got himself a sharp lawyer; I got a really dumb lawyer. When I got off the bus at the minimum-security facility, it turns out that they were waiting for me. It turns out that there was really a battle going on regarding punishment versus care and treatment. I found myself caught in the middle of this. The care-and-treatment guys wanted me to put together a show for them, but they said I had to go through a week of hard labor to satisfy the punishment guys. They made me the head of the dormitory, and I was able to go and write while these other guys went out to do the labor. That created resentment, particularly with one guard. I was the 'mother' of my particular barracks, and the 'mothers' were supposed to eat early. So when the inmates ate breakfast, the 'mothers' would straighten up the place. One morning, I show up late for breakfast, and this guard sent me off to maximum security. It was overcrowded, three guys to a cell. Arlyne, the woman I eventually married, contacted an outfit called Narcotics Anonymous, and they got my sentence modified. They came and got me out of maximum security, drove me into town to a hearing, and I was free."

Mulligan married Arlyne Brown, the daughter of songwriter Lew Brown, in May 1953, after his brief marriage to Jeffie Boyd had ended. That did not, however, end his battles with drugs. Since he had started to use heroin again after his breakup with Gail Madden, he began to look for professional help. "The attitude of the police," he recalled, "was that drug addiction was an incurable disease. By having this attitude, they helped make it a self-fulfilling prophecy. They were thoroughly rotten in most cities to drug addicts and most especially to jazz musicians."

Because of this type of atmosphere, Mulligan said, "doctors and psychiatrists were loathe to treat any addicts. They were afraid they would get in trouble and lose their licenses. I went to a number of doctors in Los Angeles and always got the same answer: If I stopped using drugs for six months, they would consider taking me on as a patient. I said, 'If I could stop taking this stuff for six months, I wouldn't need you.'"

6

'IT WAS MUCH LIKE PLAYING WITH BACH MIGHT HAVE BEEN'

Shortly after Mulligan was released from prison, he and Arlyne were walking down Hollywood Boulevard when they ran into Baker. "Chet came up to us and, I swear, he never said hello or 'Gerry, it's great to see you.' The first thing he said was, 'Gerry, I've decided I've got to have $300 a week.' I laughed. It was so outrageously off the mark. Chet never could figure out what I was laughing at. I kind of heaved a sigh of relief because, as much as it meant musically to have the group with Chet, I realized that being on the road I would be sweating blood when Chet was driving. In those days, the best-paid player in a band like Tommy Dorsey's or Harry James's was getting $250 a week."

Mulligan replaced Baker with valve trombonist Bob Brookmeyer, and that collaboration may have been foreshadowed by an earlier encounter with tenor saxophonist Stan Getz. "Stan Getz had a group very much modeled on the quartet, a contrapuntal relationship between two horns," Mulligan recalled. "The other horn with him was Bob Brookmeyer. Well, I remember we had a session in the house that Chet was renting. The four horns were Chet, Stan, Bob, and me. What a great four-horn front line it was! The four of us together were able to improvise ensemble things. It was wonderful. Stan tried to talk up the idea that we should go on the road, and it should be his band. Brookmeyer and Chet and I looked at each other and kind of rolled our eyes. I guess we all decided we didn't want to be in Stan's band, so that was the end of it musically. When you've got individuals—each one wrapped up in his own ideas and ambitions—it's very difficult to put them together. We didn't have anybody kind of helping with the direction of the group."

When he started to reorganize the quartet in January 1954, Mulligan told Brookmeyer to bring a drummer and bass player from New York. "Brookmeyer brought bassist Red Mitchell and drummer Frank Isola. I flew them out to California, we rehearsed, we played one date, and then got on a plane and flew back to New York—except I drove, because I had bought a car. That was kind of the beginning of the end of my marriage [to Arlyne], because I remember we fought all the way. Our personalities were totally unsuited to each other."

In 1957, Mulligan and Arlyne had a son, Reed Brown Mulligan, and the marriage ultimately broke up, Mulligan said, "for the sake of the child. Usually people stay together for the sake of the child. I left because a child growing up in this atmosphere of anger, tension, and constant turmoil was not good." Reed was two years old when Mulligan and Arlyne divorced. He lived in New York with his mother, and Mulligan would visit him when in the city.

Asked what it was like to play with Mulligan, Brookmeyer's response in *Listen: Gerry Mulligan* was: "It was much like playing with Bach might have been. The strength of his lines—he always seemed to have the right lines at the right place, right time, right way."

In June 1954, the quartet with Brookmeyer, Mitchell, and Isola made a triumphant appearance in Paris, playing at the Salle Pleyel. Claude Carriere, in the liner notes to *Gerry Mulligan in Paris*—reissued on RCA Records' Disque Vogue label in 1995—attempted to re-create the atmosphere.

"This Mulligan music," he wrote, "held an immediate appeal, conquering Paris audiences from the very first concert." The audiences were familiar with the Mulligan-Baker pianoless quartet, he said, but "the new frontline voicing of baritone sax and valve trombone proved just as acceptable, all the more so since both soloists—each also an excellent composer and arranger—displayed such total ease and relaxation. The breathtaking mastery of harmony and counterpoint soon made listeners forget the absence of a piano. Moreover, the rhythm section Mulligan had brought to

Paris played a by-no-means negligible role in the considerable success the quartet enjoyed."

AllMusic's Scott Yanow, reviewing the Paris reissue, felt the unit of Mulligan, Brookmeyer, Mitchell, and Isola "was one of Jeru's finest, for his own wit, swing, and cool-toned creativity were matched by Brookmeyer." Yanow singled out "Walkin' Shoes," "Love Me or Leave Me," "My Funny Valentine," and "Five Brothers" as highlights on the two-disc album, but added that "Every selection is quite enjoyable. The audience is rightfully enthusiastic."

Doug Ramsey, reviewing two previously unreleased performances of the Mulligan Quartet with Brookmeyer in the June 2001 issue of *Jazz Times*, said the recordings "demonstrate the vitality and swing the horn players generated and the sophistication and chance-taking that increased the longer they stayed together." Ramsey described a 1957 Hollywood Bowl concert performance of the Jule Styne/Sammy Cahn tune "Come Out, Come Out, Wherever You Are" as "counterpoint with Brookmeyer as uncanny as Mulligan's intertwining lines with Chet Baker in the original quartet, and more joyous . . . During his Mulligan period, Brookmeyer was making full use of his repertoire of smears, growls, shouts, and half-valve chokes. The effects were not gimmicks. He worked them into his hybrid style of traditionalist verve, bebop complexity, and original harmonic thinking to become an ideal foil for what has been called Mulligan's old-time modern playing. The two players constructed improvised lines that exposed them for what they were: superb composers, collaborating in instantaneous compositions."

When the quartet was booked to play Storyville, the Boston club run by Newport Jazz Festival founder George Wein, Mulligan met Wein for the first time, forging a relationship that would remain strong throughout the musician's career. "I really liked Storyville," Mulligan said. "It was a great club. It was a dinner restaurant and very classy-looking on the first floor. Then downstairs in this hotel was another room, smaller like a saloon, and they called that Mahogany Hall. Down there, he had traditional bands. We'd be playing upstairs, and maybe playing downstairs would be Jimmy McPartland and Vic Dickenson and Pee Wee Russell. You'd meet all these wonderful guys, and we would have a grand time in the place. It was a wonderful atmosphere." During the engagement, *Down Beat*'s Bob Martin wrote that the quartet's performance was "one of the most comfortably swinging weeks in the club's history."

A unique characteristic of Mulligan was his ability to embrace all styles of jazz, regardless of his own particular specialty. Alto saxophonist Paul Desmond told Nat Hentoff in the March 21, 1959 *New Yorker* article that, "In probably no other jazz instrumentalist, can you find such a clear progression from Dixieland thru swing and into and out of bebop, all on the same record, if not in the same solo."

Hentoff expanded on Mulligan's flexibility in *Jazz Is*. By the late '50s, he said, Mulligan had become "the Johnny Appleseed of jam sessions, using any playing opportunity he could find to get a session going. At one of the Newport Jazz Festival evenings, for instance, he was scheduled to play only once, but he ended up playing half a dozen times, onstage and later at jam sessions and parties, including one given by impresario Norman Granz, that produced the most spontaneous jazz of the Festival."

Mulligan "had no qualms about sitting in with anybody," said bassist Bill Crow. "He would walk on when Charlie Parker was playing and take his horn out on the stage. But the thing is, he could play that well, so nobody thought it was an intrusion. He was always invited to the party because they knew he was a good jam session player."

Wein told me that Mulligan simply "loved the traditions of jazz. He translated those traditions into a more modern style. He always did one thing: He always knew where the melody was." Mulligan's appreciation for the traditions of jazz endured throughout his career. In a January 1989 interview with *Down Beat*'s Michael Bourne, he talked about the importance of young musicians having a sense of history. "One of the things I liked about jazz," he said, "was that there was a tradition going on, and I liked the tradition. I admired very much the musicians who went before: Louis Armstrong, Jack Teagarden, the bandleaders, the writers, Sy Oliver, wonderful people like that."

This appreciation for history and tradition was a key reason Mulligan loved the atmosphere of Wein's Newport Jazz Festival. "At Newport," Mulligan said, "you ended up playing with a lot of different groups, from different eras and different styles. That was something George wanted to do. He knew I liked to do it. Newport was a lot of fun, especially in the early years. We'd have jam sessions, and I'd find myself on the stage with

Coleman Hawkins and Vic Dickenson, kind of an unbelievable collection of players."

Social connections between musicians were very important to Mulligan, and Newport, he said, "had that. We had time to spend together and hang out, talk about ideas—the give and take of natural social relationships. And I'd also rehearse new stuff with my group, or guys would get together with musicians they wanted to do something with but wouldn't have time otherwise. So in that way, it was wonderful. Those early days of Newport showed great promise of what we expected the future to hold. We introduced the quartet with Art Farmer there. I would wind up spending time with Cannonball Adderley, who was a wonderful guy. I had such admiration for him as a person as well as a player. And, of course, I spent a lot of time with Paul Desmond. I ended up hanging out with him for days and regretting it because I always drank too much. Another person I used to enjoy hanging out with was Johnny Mercer. We always talked about doing a project together, which I really wanted to do."

There was one occasion, at the first Newport Jazz Festival, in 1954, when Mulligan's spontaneity irritated Wein. "I'd worked so hard to put together a reunion of Billie Holiday, Teddy Wilson, Lester Young, Buck Clayton, and Jo Jones," Wein recalled. "It was re-creating the great Billie Holiday bands of the '30s—the first great records she made. And Gerry was so moved by that, he jumped up on the stage to play with them. And I didn't want him on the stage. I was really upset at that time. He disrupted the memory-feeling of what I was trying to get. But he wanted to be part of it. At his funeral, I talked about how I was very mad at him, but now I see that he belonged there, because they're all up in Valhalla together. And I'm sure they're playing together, so I forgive him."

Mulligan would have another opportunity to play at a Holiday-Young reunion on *The Sound of Jazz,* the groundbreaking jazz television program put together by Nat Hentoff and another prominent jazz writer, Whitney Balliett, which was telecast live on CBS in 1957. Young was in ill health and remained seated during a performance with Holiday of a song she had written, "Fine and Mellow." Mulligan played the first solo, followed by Ben Webster on tenor sax. Then, according to Hentoff (in *Jazz: A History of America's Music* by Geoffrey C. Ward and Ken Burns), "Lester got up, and he played the purest blues I have ever heard . . ."

Being part of *The Sound of Jazz*, Mulligan remembered, was "like being a kid in a candy store. I found myself playing with the Count Basie Band with as many of the old players as they could get." Playing behind Holiday, he said, was "a high point for me. That was one of the most touching moments of anything I've done on film. When they do the close-up of Billie's face, I start playing a solo, and the camera's on me, and you see her face and her reaction—man! It brings tears trickling down my cheeks on that one. She has such as sweet, serene look and a kind of Mona Lisa smile; it just puts me away." "Though no one could have known it then," wrote Ward and Burns, "*The Sound of Jazz* remains the high-water mark of jazz on American television." Mulligan recalled, "It was a lovely moment, an incredibly fulfilling experience on television."

Meanwhile, Mulligan's quartet with Brookmeyer had been well received at Storyville. "For whatever reason," Mulligan said, "people responded very well to us, kind of an instant acceptance wherever we went with it. A lot of the stuff was written in the lowest register, and Brookmeyer was always conscious of the fact that we had to have two low voices instead of a high one. It wasn't just a replacement for Chet; it was a different band. It was a good enough band that people accepted it on its own terms."

Jazz historian Bill Kirchner (writing in the liner notes to *The Complete Verve Gerry Mulligan Concert Jazz Band Sessions*) believes that "as musically superb—and commercially successful—as the pairing of Mulligan and Baker had been, this new combination proved at least as spectacular, and much longer in duration."

In his *New Yorker* article, Hentoff recalled a performance by the Mulligan-Brookmeyer quartet at Newport. "The large tawny voice of Mulligan's horn," he wrote, "contrasted, but did not clash, with the more burnished, more gently burred singing of Brookmeyer's." Hentoff also referred to an interview with Brookmeyer in Britain's *Melody Maker* magazine, in which the trombonist said, "I think, in time, [Mulligan] will rise to the stature of people like Duke Ellington."

When Mulligan and Brookmeyer were reunited for a performance in Toronto in 1965, the *Toronto Telegram*'s Helen McNamara wrote that "the rapport between Mulligan and Brookmeyer is most evident, especially when they comment on each other's solos, sometimes with a staggering humor or soft aside . . . The quartet achieves even more variety when both men take turns at piano, an instrument that offers them still another means of indulging their considerable improvising talents."

While the original quartet with Baker was still together, Mulligan had put together a tentette that recorded one album on Capitol in 1953 (*Gerry Mulligan and His Ten-Tette*, reissued in 2008 by DRG). The tentette, he said, "was based on the *Birth of the Cool* nonet instrumentation. The main difference was that I added a baritone saxophone. I had two baritones playing with the ensemble, so I was freed up for more of a solo role. And I could do more things like the quartet, trumpet and baritone. That gave an extra dimension to the possibilities of arranging." Another change was that the trumpet playing was split between Baker and Pete Candoli. "I always thought," said Mulligan, "that in the *Birth of the Cool* band, we could have used a second trumpet. Miles was always able to carry that off, but he had his horn in his face a lot during the course of the night. He played solos, and he played lead; and he was playing backgrounds. I wanted to split those chores."

Mulligan felt the album, originally produced by Gene Norman, "came out very well," but the tentette was short-lived. "We didn't have much rehearsal time," he recalled, "and often there wasn't that much recording time. I had a couple of three-hour recording sessions, and a certain number of things had to be done. One of the things you learn as an arranger, composer, bandleader, or soloist—everything costs money." That's why, he added, "when I get into rehearsal—no matter who's paying for it—that's a luxury. You'll never see me wasting time schmoozing or hanging out."

Writing about *Gerry Mulligan and His Ten-Tette* on InternetFM.com, Eric Berman acknowledged the influence of *Birth of the Cool* on the tentette's playing. But, he added, "Even though the tentette recordings are less well known than the storied *Birth of the Cool* sessions, they are every bit as essential and influential." Berman also recounted a 1971 comment by Mulligan about the short-lived tentette: "I would have liked to pursue (the tentette) further at the time," Mulligan said, "but c'est la vie."

There was also a relatively brief sextet comprised of trumpeters Jon Eardley or Don Ferrara, tenor saxophonist Zoot Sims, and Brookmeyer, plus bass and drums. Whitney Balliett, in *A Journal of Jazz 1954–2000*, described it as "partly written, partly jammed music built on unison or free-flowing ensembles, solos backed by organ chords or Ellington melodic fragments, and a clear, uncluttered rhythmic pulse . . . It was a dense, swinging music, and when the four horns took off at the end of a number for several choruses of collective soloing, audiences found themselves shouting and jumping."

Gordon Jack, in *Fifties Jazz Talk*, said Mulligan's "expertise as a composer of improvised arrangements was particularly evident" in the sextet, "what many consider to be his best ever small group . . . He takes on his customary role of a Pied Piper, leading Brookmeyer, Zoot Sims, and Don Ferrara through a series of extemporaneous riffs, hinting at a phrase here and a comment there, which, in turn, is picked up by the other horns and developed into what could almost be a written arrangement."

Wein remembered playing piano with the sextet. "Gerry was coming up for a date in Storyville. I said, 'Put the band together. I'll play for you.' He had a whole week to get that group together, and he was happy because he had a chance to write for more horns than just the quartet. I always put him in many different instrumentations and always let him do what he would like to do."

The sextet lasted about a year and a half—from mid-1955 until the end of 1956. Balliett speculated about the reason for its brevity. "Mulligan was heady and restless at the time, and, because the public response was limited, or there weren't enough jobs, or he wanted to get on with other things, he dissolved the group."

In 1957, Brookmeyer left the Mulligan quartet and was replaced by trumpeter Art Farmer. Although that version of the quartet—with Henry Grimes or Bill Crow on bass and Dave Bailey on drums—stayed together for less than two years, Mulligan said it "was one of my favorite quartets. Art brought a totally different kind of approach, and the arrangements that evolved were altogether different. Art had said that it was difficult for him working without a piano and working with these tightly knit arrangements. I was constantly playing harmony, taking over the role of the piano. It was a big adjustment for other players to come into that setup. But when they established rapport, it was great."

In *Listen: Gerry Mulligan*, Farmer recalled that first appearance with the quartet in Westbury, New York. "My previous group," he said, "had been led by pianist Horace Silver, a very strong pianist. And suddenly, I find myself with this group that doesn't have a pianist. But when I got up onstage to play with the quartet, and the quartet started playing, I felt like I was in a dream, like you're walking down the street with no clothes on." Russ Wilson, reviewing the Mulligan-Farmer quartet for the *Oakland Tribune,* said it created "a glittery array of tone colors, a fascinating deployment of counterpoint and some brilliant solos, all marked by a most infectious swing."

Each one of the quartets in the '50s, Mulligan pointed out, "was different. What Chet and I did was one thing. What Bob and I did was another thing altogether, and the things with Art were totally different. There were things that came out of each group that were something special. I probably wrote more for that [Farmer] group. What I was trying to achieve with that group was that the written things shouldn't sound written. With the other groups, it was often the other way around—we would play head things that sounded arranged."

Bill Crow remembered getting a call from Mulligan about joining the quartet with Farmer. "I was delighted to go back with Gerry," he said. "We stayed together for about a year. We did a European tour. We played Newport a couple of times. And then Dave Bailey called me up one day and said, 'Gerry's got a movie. He asked for the quartet to be in it. And they're offering us $400 a week.' I didn't really want to go to California. A week later, Dave called and said, 'Pack your bag. They just raised the ante to $750.' I had already made plans to do something else, so I turned it down. If I had gone out there, I would probably never have married my wife, Eileen. I didn't hear anything more from Gerry until the Concert Jazz Band came through. Then it was time to go back to work with him. That is the best band I ever played with."

The movie was *I Want to Live!,* directed by Robert Wise and about convicted murderess Barbara Graham. Susan Hayward's portrayal of Graham won Hayward an Academy Award for best actress. Wise was known as a director who liked to make music an essential part of his movies, and André Previn recommended that he hire Johnny Mandel to write the score. Mandel and Mulligan knew each other from their early big-band days, but there was another compelling reason to hire Mulligan for the movie: According to the liner notes for the original MGM Music soundtrack to *I Want to Live!,* Graham was "actually a big Mulligan fan. She even played the baritone saxophonist's records while in the death house. In the film, as she listens to a radio in her cell, Graham remarks, 'That's Gerry Mulligan.' 'How do you know?' asks a prison attendant. 'I have all his records,' she declares." Mandel hired Mulligan's quartet to appear on camera in the opening scene and to play throughout the soundtrack.

In a radio interview on WNCN-FM in New York in April 1960, Leonard Feather asked Mulligan if he thought *I Want to Live!* had gotten the recognition it deserved for its musical achievements. The answer was a clear 'no.' "The fact that they not only didn't give Johnny Mandel an Oscar, but didn't even nominate him," Mulligan responded, "just convinces me of the closed doors, the private little club that the movie composers have. And they say this is the first movie music Johnny wrote. Actually, it's just the first he ever got credit for—a good part of the good jazz music that was heard in segments of other pictures was written by Johnny. They call that ghosting."

Farmer appeared with Mulligan in the film and then moved on to form the Jazztet, a sextet with tenor saxophonist Benny Golson. "For a player like Art," Mulligan recalled, "the quartet always presented something like a straitjacket. It was not the kind of free-blowing situation that you get with a regular rhythm section."

In December 1957, there was a brief reunion with Chet Baker to record an album on the World Pacific label, appropriately called *Reunion*, with Henry Grimes on bass and Dave Bailey on drums. *Coda*'s David Lewis, in the January 2, 1998 issue, called the recording "brilliant . . . This band shows how Baker and Mulligan had evolved into superior soloists in just three years." AllMusic's Scott Yanow, pointing out that Mulligan and Baker "had very few reunions after 1953," said, "this particular CD from 1957 is an exception. Although not quite possessing the magic of the earlier group, the music is quite enjoyable, and the interplay between the two horns is still special."

Although the exact timing isn't clear, sometime during the late '50s, Mulligan finally beat his drug habit. "I had taken a group out on the road," he said, "and one of the guys with us on the trip wanted to try heroin. I tried to talk him out of it, but he got it and came back to the hotel and turned himself on and proceeded to pass out. I had some experience with guys passing out, and, between Zoot [Sims] and me, we'd saved the lives of a lot of guys because we worked on them until we revived them. I wound up spending the night giving this player artificial respiration. The next day, I decided I'd simply had it. I didn't want to have anything more to do with any of it. We were in Detroit and were supposed to go to Chicago next. I called my agent and said, 'Cancel out Chicago. Don't book me with this group anymore, and if you want me, I'll be in the hospital. I put myself in a clinic in New York for a couple of weeks, and that was the end of it."

Mulligan described this period as "a slow process of getting through my own emotional turmoils and whatever it was that made reality so unbearable that heroin wasn't the desirable agent of forgetfulness. I was lucky to find a psychiatrist who would take me on, and I stuck with him. I don't remember when I started with him, and I don't remember how long I was with him. Once I kicked it, I was anxious to get back to work. It was hard for a while, because when you're able to turn to a quick fix to take the bad feelings away, you get used to the idea. Physically, I felt great, so I did a lot of stuff during that period of the late '50s."

7

'WE WERE ALL IN LOVE WITH JUDY'

"It was 1939, and the Village Vanguard was four years old. There were nights when I'd sit in the back and talk to a pretty, shy, blonde girl, sixteen, maybe seventeen years old, who used to hang out in the place. She'd come in with a guy, or with another girl, or alone. She hung out in the Village, like a lot of other kids, because she could breathe more freely, so to speak, than uptown, where she lived with her mother. I learned that her name was Judy."

—Max Gordon in *Live at the Village Vanguard*

Judy Tuvim was the young girl who hung out at the Village Vanguard. Owner Max Gordon gave her and some of her friends—who included the future songwriting team of Betty Comden and Adolph Green—an opportunity to perform at the Vanguard as a group known as the Revuers. Tuvim, who changed her last name to Holliday (*tuvim* was the Hebrew word for "holiday"), rose to stardom in 1946 as the lead in Garson Kanin's Broadway play *Born Yesterday*. Ironically, Jean Arthur had been scheduled to play the part but became ill three days before the play was to open in Philadelphia.

In the late '50s, Judy Holliday was an established star. She had won an Academy Award for Best Actress in the 1950 movie version of *Born Yesterday* and had been featured in such other movies as *It Should Happen to You*, *Phffft*, and *The Solid Gold Cadillac*. In 1956, she received a Tony Award for her performance in the Broadway musical *Bells Are Ringing*.

Mulligan was back in New York in the late '50s, and would later remember himself during that time as "kind of a bachelor or a loose cannon, depending on how you look at it. I met a lot of nice ladies during that period, some of whom I spent more time with than others. Then, I was invited to party at the house of the Broadway director Bobby Lewis (*Brigadoon*, *Teahouse of the August Moon*). I go to this party, and Judy Holliday showed up. I recognized her, and, at some point in the evening, Judy and I started talking. She knew who I was, and she loved music. So we got along really great. She invited me to the theater, and a couple of nights later I went down to the theater and backstage to see her. We started meeting after the show (*Bells Are Ringing*) and going out to eat. Then, I took an apartment near her on 72nd Street. She had an apartment in the Dakota and a place she had gotten with her ex-husband in upstate New York (Washingtonville)."

While Holliday was still appearing in *Bells Are Ringing*, Mulligan was playing with his quartet at a New York club, when he was visited by movie director Vincente Minnelli and producer Arthur Freed. "Arthur spoke about a project that he was doing," Mulligan said. "He wanted to make a film of the Jack Kerouac book *The Subterraneans.* He wanted a musician to play one of the characters in the film, and he was curious to meet me because he felt he and Minnelli may have used my name inadvertently for the character Gene Kelly played in *An American in Paris*. I said, 'Sure, I'd like to try it,' and I agreed to do the film. Judy was still doing *Bells Are Ringing* on Broadway, and the filming of *Bells* was supposed to start in February of the following year. Things kept getting postponed, and the shooting time for *Bells* turned out to be at the same time as the shooting of *The Subterraneans.*"

Kerouac's semifictional novella told the story of his short romance with a black woman; for the movie, the character was changed into a French woman, played by Leslie Caron. The film's reviews were lukewarm at best, but the soundtrack, composed and conducted by André Previn, was much more warmly received. Mulligan appeared in the movie as a priest who played the saxophone and was joined by an all-star roster of musicians, some of whom played themselves onscreen. They included vocalist Carmen McRae, drummer Shelly Manne, and bassist Red Mitchell. Previn, according to the Screen Archives Entertainment website, "was the ideal composer to pull off such a marriage: at once a classically trained musician who scored a bevy of high-profile pictures for MGM in the 1950s, he was also a talented jazz pianist who soaked up the atmosphere of the West Coast jazz movement—all at 31 years of age."

Mulligan's performance as the priest, Joshua Hoskins, elicited at least one positive mention. A. H. Weiler, writing in the July 7, 1960 issue of *The New York Times*, was less than enthusiastic about the performances of the leads, Caron and George Peppard, but he noted that "Roddy McDowall, Jim Hutton, Scott Marlowe, Arte Johnson, and Gerry Mulligan, as a saxophone-playing preacher, add a few passing interesting touches as the bizarre, leading types in this beatnik circle."

Meanwhile, the filming of *Bells Are Ringing*, also being made by Freed and Minnelli, turned out to be a very difficult ordeal for Holliday. "For a change," Mulligan said, "I was in the position of being able to help somebody, instead of somebody helping me. She had done the show on Broadway for two years and then did it on the road in San Francisco and Los Angeles. By the time they finally got around to doing the film, she was having doubts about doing it because there was a basic problem with the show, and she felt the writers hadn't solved that problem. *Bells* was a little show, based around a character that Judy played (a telephone answering service operator who falls in love with one of her clients). It was charming onstage because of what Judy brought to it. She brought the character and the whole show to life. But it really was a very slim show, and when you open this up as a film, you realize there's not much of a story there. They wound up trying to make an extravaganza out of a little show. The movie Freed and Minnelli had done before that was *Gigi*, a big, colorful extravaganza all over Paris. This was absolutely the opposite. The main action took place more or less on one set, a room in a New York brownstone. There weren't many people involved, and there wasn't any way of opening it up."

A few days before the shooting started, Minnelli invited Holliday and Mulligan to his house, which was near the Beverly Hills Hotel. "You go through these gates," Mulligan recalled, "and it's like being in another world. Minnelli couldn't have been more charming. Liza was there; I guess she was twelve or thirteen. He assured Judy he'd do everything to make her comfortable. They were to meet for the first day of shooting the following

Monday, and Judy had assurance from someone that they were not going to go in and start shooting right away, that they were going to go in and have a couple of days of rehearsals, reading through the script because about half of the people in the movie were not in the stage show. When doing comedy, so much is dependent on timing and chemistry between people, so Judy really felt it was necessary to rehearse."

When the shooting started, any semblance of chemistry between Holliday and Minnelli quickly disappeared. "Vincente had been kindness and friendship personified before they started shooting," Mulligan recalled. "When they got into the actual shooting, he became very short with her. She had done this onstage for two and a half years, so there were lots of things they did onstage that were not in the script. She would tell him, 'Well, something that really got a laugh onstage would be . . .' and Minnelli would always look unconvinced and would say, 'Well, show me.' She would do stuff out of context, and it really was awkward. He would stand with a pained look on his face and say, 'Why is that funny?' This happened a lot until, finally, she wouldn't make any suggestions."

It seemed to the actors, Mulligan said, that Minnelli "spent much more time rehearsing the camera than he did with the actors. They'd sometimes take a whole morning, and sometimes a whole day, just setting up the camera shots. All of the actors were very uncomfortable because of the way they were working. The script girl took Judy aside and said, 'It's obvious that Mr. Minnelli is not going to take any of your suggestions, so, let's try something. If you tell me your suggestions, then I'll say it like it's my idea, and we'll see if we can get some of the things you want into what we're doing.' Judy was willing to try it, and it worked. But as the shooting went on, it became more and more obvious to Judy that the film had lost its connection with the original show. She started to get more and more upset. I think poor Arthur Freed was really in the middle."

Holliday was so upset with the rough cut of the film that she decided to reedit it herself. "I tried to talk her out of it," Mulligan said, "but she wanted to do it, so I thought I had to back her up. When we got it done, the picture was quite different from the finished film. Arthur said he was obliged to show it to Vincente, and Vincente was furious and demanded that it be disassembled immediately. That was kind of the last straw as far as the relationship between Judy and Arthur; I think Arthur just wanted the thing over. When the picture came out, Judy didn't really like it at all because it was kind of rambling, and she felt she didn't look good. And that fixed my reputation in Hollywood. I was a troublemaker."

In a synopsis of the film by Margarita Landazuri on TCM.com, Mulligan is actually credited with being a positive influence. Pointing out that cast and crew were "gentle and considerate" with Holliday, Landazuri added that "she was somewhat calmed by the presence of her new boyfriend, jazz musician and sometime actor Gerry Mulligan, who played her blind date in the film."

Despite all the acrimony that existed during the filming of the movie, there were some uplifting memories. Holliday had rented a large house for her mother and son, and "just about every week, we'd have guys over for a jam session. Ben [Webster] and Quincy [Jones] came, and we'd have Mel Lewis on drums, Jimmy Rowles on piano, and Leroy [Vinnegar] on bass. And it was great."

Mulligan also did a guest spot on *The Dinah Shore Show*. "Dinah," he said, "was great. I really liked her. She was down to earth, no crap. Frank Sinatra was also on the show. We rehearsed the show, and we did our part of it. Dinah was getting upset because Frank wasn't there, and she knew that Frank didn't like to rehearse. Then he arrives with these two giant bodyguards with him. Dinah goes over and says, 'Frank, I'd like you to meet Gerry Mulligan,' and the bodyguard steps between us, and they just walk right by me. Dinah looks at me and rolls her eyes. That was just so strange. I always admired him as a singer, but I always had reservations about him personally after that."

Bells Are Ringing premiered at Radio City Music Hall, and, according to Landazuri, it opened "to huge crowds and even better reviews than the play had received. It broke Music Hall records, grossing over a million dollars in its seven-week run. But that was New York, and *Bells Are Ringing* was a New York musical. The rest of the country couldn't have cared less. It was Minnelli's least profitable film since *The Pirate* (1948)."

After *Bells Are Ringing*, Holliday was signed to do her first dramatic role for a Broadway show called *Laurette*, based on the life of Laurette Taylor, an actress who was popular in the first half of the 20th century but who battled with alcoholism. Holliday was on the road in the pre-Broadway run when Mulligan received a phone call from one of her friends saying that a doctor, examining Judy for insurance for the show, had found a lump in her breast, and she had to go into the hospital immediately. Mulligan had been playing a gig in Santa Monica but flew back to New York. "Judy tried to talk them into letting her play the part one more time," Mulligan recalled, "but a surgeon did a radical mastectomy, and that finished her and the show for quite a while. It was hard to get her to move out of the house at all. I was with her through the operation. The psychological effect on her was devastating. It was a long uphill battle to get her to just face life at all."

Holliday died in 1965, but, during the five-year period from her initial diagnosis to her death, Mulligan stayed with her, and they collaborated musically. "This period," Mulligan recalled, "was probably the most severe learning experience that I went through, to be able to get a handle on what's important in life. It was obviously a difficult time."

During this time, Mulligan and Holliday collaborated on songwriting, with Holliday writing lyrics to Mulligan's music. Mulligan had been contacted by the playwright Anita Loos (best known for writing *Gentlemen Prefer Blondes*) about writing music for a musical adaptation of *Happy Birthday*, her hit Broadway play from the late 1940s. "Anita Loos was on some kind of symposium program on television," Mulligan said, "and Nat Hentoff was on it, too. One of the subjects that came up was the music of the theater: 'Where are the new writers coming from?' Nat said he thought the theater was missing a bet by not tapping into the talent that was on the jazz scene. He thought there were people in jazz who would do well in the theater. Anita said, 'Who?' and Nat said, 'For one, Gerry Mulligan.' So, she got my number from Nat and called me up and asked me if I'd be interested in writing music for a comedy/play she had written. I said, 'Sure,' so I met with her, and she showed me the play, *Happy Birthday*, which she'd written for Helen Hayes." The play revolved around a librarian, played by Hayes, who is in love with a bank clerk and gets drunk to release her true feelings. The play ran for seventeen months, and Hayes won a Tony Award for Best Actress, but Loos told Mulligan it was never made into a movie because the Hollywood censors felt it glorified drinking.

"She said she had always dreamed of making a musical out of it," Mulligan recalled, "but it needed rewriting. Then she asked if there was anyone I wanted to write lyrics with me. I said Judy Holliday was a friend of mine, we'd written things together; and she was a first-rate lyricist. She said that would be great, and maybe Judy would be interested to play the role also. I said that was her decision to make. So it was kind of a lark."

Bill Crow remembered those days. "We were all in love with Judy," he said. "Gerry and Judy were a happy couple. They wrote songs that reflected that happiness. Judy had a flair for writing lyrics. My wife and I spent an evening at Judy's house in Washingtonville where she sang all the songs, with Gerry at the piano. Judy recorded some of the songs they wrote for *Happy Birthday* on a studio album with an augmented version of Gerry's big band." Elliot Lawrence by then had become a Broadway conductor, and he recalled receiving a phone call from Mulligan: "'Elliot,' he said, 'I'd like you to come over because Judy and I are working on a Broadway show. I know this is your field.' I said, 'Of course.' Judy Holliday was one of my favorite singers. I went to her apartment. Gerry was at the piano. Judy sang four or five songs. It was a marvelous afternoon. I liked the songs, and I encouraged them."

According to Crow, Holliday was unhappy with her singing, and there were plans to redo some of the songs, but she died before that could be done. The album was eventually released in 1980 by DRG Records as *Holliday with Mulligan.* It contained four Mulligan-Holiday originals—"What's the Rush," "Loving You," "It Must Be Christmas," and "Summer's Over"—along with several standards, such as Irving Berlin's "Supper Time" and Harold Arlen and Ted Koehler's "I Gotta Right to Sing the Blues."

Mulligan recalled that "the idea of making a record made her so nervous. She had done another date for CBS (Columbia) called 'Trouble Is a Man.' She'd go to the ladies room and heave, and then she'd be back ready to sing. She was such a great performer onstage, but getting started was murder. But we decided to do the album so we could record some of these things we had written. The big band wasn't the ideal accompaniment, but she and I liked having a band where she was the band singer. So I wound up having an instrumentation that was very close to being what became the Concert Jazz Band: three trumpets, and, instead of having three trombones, I had three French horns, four reeds, and piano, bass, and drums."

Scott Yanow, reviewing the album for AllMusic, thought the big band was "largely wasted" on the recording, but did believe the record featured Holliday "doing some effective singing." Pointing out that Mulligan and Holliday were "an 'item' around the time of this recording," Yanow added that the album is "of greater historical value than of interest to jazz listeners."

Happy Birthday the musical never made it to the Broadway stage, apparently because of problems with rewriting the script, which were never resolved. However, it did reach the stage in December 1974 at the University of Alabama at Birmingham. "Anita had a friend at the town-and-gown theater affiliated with the university," Mulligan said, "and she asked if I was interested in doing it. We did a week's worth of performances, with Fannie Flagg in the leading role. I brought a couple of musicians with me, including Tom Fay, who was playing piano with me and was helping me with a lot of the writing. It was an adventure, but it was worth it to finally see this thing on its feet and to realize the songs really were good. I wish Judy could have seen it."

The relationship with Holliday had a lasting effect on Mulligan. "Because of the way Judy was," he said, "I wound up learning a lot about how to be with another person. I'd always been so self-centered and totally focused on music. Dealing with Judy, I started to become conscious of somebody else's problems. Suddenly, the most important thing in life became being a crutch for her, to help her cope with problems as they arose." Holliday, he said, was very discouraged about being typecast as "the dumb blonde." "She tried very hard to get them to write stuff for her that had other dimensions to it," he said, but, "naturally, in Hollywood, they kept trying to write the same character over and over again. She was capable of a lot more, so it was frustrating for her."

One time in New York, Mulligan took Holliday to Birdland to hear Cannonball Adderley. "She thought it was an enviable quality that musicians appreciated when someone else played great. She thought it was so different than the theater, where people were depressed when somebody else did something good. This was one of the things about the jazz scene that really struck her. She really felt a tremendous kinship with the music, with the players, and with the scene."

Early in her film career, Holliday had received unexpected support from Katharine Hepburn. Before *Born Yesterday*, she had appeared in *Adam's Rib* with Hepburn and Spencer Tracy. Normally, said Mulligan, "Katharine

Gerry Mulligan (*right*) with his brothers at Christmas, 1930.

Gerry with his father, 1930 or '31.

Gerry's parents, Louise and George Mulligan, 1932.

Gerry, 1934.

TOP: *Birth of the Cool. From left*: Miles Davis, Lee Konitz, and Gerry Mulligan.

LEFT: Gerry, *center*, with Chet Baker, *left*, and Lee Konitz, *right*, in 1953.

From left: Jimmy Cleveland, Gerry, Bill Crow, and Art Farmer, 1956.

Gerry with Anita O'Day at the Newport Jazz Festival in 1957.

The Sound of Jazz on CBS. *From left*: Ben Webster, Earle Warren, Lester Young, and Gerry.

Gerry Mulligan Sextet in Amsterdam, 1957. At far left is Bob Brookmeyer; second from right is Zoot Sims.

Gerry at the piano with, *from left*, Teddy Wilson, Dizzy Gillespie, and Miles Davis, 1958.

Judy Holliday and Gerry recording *Holliday with Mulligan*, 1961.

On tour with Dave Brubeck, in the late '60s or early '70s.

Recording *Summit* with Astor Piazzolla, 1974.

Rehearsing for the 1974 Carnegie Hall Chet Baker reunion concert. *From left*: Ron Carter, Gerry, Dave Samuels, and John Scofield.

Gerry and Chet Baker, rehearsing for the '74 reunion concert.

On tour with Stan Getz's All-Star Band in Germany, 1976.

Gerry and Franca, 1976.
Photo by Hank O'Neal.

Recording the soundtrack of *La Menace* with Don Elliott, 1977.

With President Jimmy Carter at a White House jazz concert in 1978.

From left: Sue Mingus, Billy Taylor, Gerry, and Charlie Mingus at a 1978 White House jazz concert.

Jamming with New York City Mayor Ed Koch, *center*, and Benny Goodman in 1979.

THE CITY OF NEW YORK
OFFICE OF THE MAYOR
NEW YORK, N.Y. 10007

July 10, 1979

Mr. Gerry Mulligan
c/o ROTA Apt.24F
20 Waterside Plaza
New York, New York 10010

Dear Gerry:

An artist spends his life studying and working on his craft -- the performance is the part the world benefits from. However, from your spontaneous session at the City's first Live From Gracie Mansion Concert, I benefited, as a trio player between two greats.

Thank you. All the best.

Sincerely,

Edward I. Koch
MAYOR

mt
encl.

Letter to Gerry from Ed Koch, 1979. Koch played saxophone with Gerry and Benny Goodman at Gracie Mansion. In his letter he said, "I benefited, as a trio player between two greats."

Hepburn refused to give interviews, particularly the press conference interview that was the staple of the Hollywood publicity department. When they were doing *Adam's Rib*, they asked her to do one of these things, and, surprisingly, she agreed. And all she would talk about was Judy. She was trying to give Judy the recognition and the boost. It was a charming thing to do." The movie was directed by George Cukor, who was known, Mulligan pointed out, "for turning the camera on and letting it go. Judy and Hepburn did this scene, and the conversation went on and on. It was a really great example of actors performing at their best. It's a great scene."

Holliday's last Broadway play was a musical called *Hot Spot*, with music and lyrics by Mary Rodgers and Martin Charnin. It opened in April 1963, but it ran for only forty-three performances. "I was on the road," Mulligan recalled. "She always said if I had been there when they played the score, I would have advised her not to do it." After that, Holliday's cancer returned, and she was no longer able to work. "The day she died," Mulligan said, "Paul Desmond and Herb Gardner, my best friends, took me in tow and hung out with me until I had adjusted to the worst of the shock."

8

'WE COULDN'T BELIEVE HOW GOOD THE BAND WAS'

Around the time Mulligan met Judy Holliday, he was also beginning to organize his first concert jazz band.

The timing couldn't have been better. *Metronome* magazine, according to Gordon Jack in *Fifties Jazz*, "organized a readers' poll in 1959 to find the most popular jazz musicians of all time." Mulligan, he said, "finished third, behind Miles Davis and the winner, Charlie Parker. The fact that Louis Armstrong and Duke Ellington finished no higher than sixth and sixteenth, respectively, shows how ephemeral polls can be, but nevertheless, it indicates how incredibly popular Mulligan was by now . . ."

"I always wanted to have a big band," Mulligan said, "and this band kind of evolved out of my various smaller groups. But if it hadn't been for the pressure from some of my friends, I probably wouldn't have put the band together. Nick Travis, a trumpet player, had been a friend of mine for a long time. I had met him when we were still in high school in Philadelphia. He began to pressure me. 'C'mon, man,' he'd say, 'you always said you wanted to have a big band. Now's the time.' And [Bob] Brookmeyer liked the idea."

The instrumentation was three trumpets; Brookmeyer's valve trombone plus two slide trombones; four reeds—clarinet, alto sax, tenor sax, and baritone sax—plus Mulligan's solo baritone; and a rhythm section of bass and drums. Occasionally, Mulligan or Brookmeyer would sit in at piano.

The bands of the '30s, Mulligan pointed out, "were much more fleet—they could move with more agility because they didn't have all that weight. I decided to try to take a smaller band and try to go back to the fleetness that I liked in an ensemble. In some ways, I thought I could do something that reminded me of the *Birth of the Cool* instrumentation." The Concert Jazz Band was also, in Mulligan's view, "part of a general movement to do more obvious things with counterpoint. The contrapuntal idea had always been there. It certainly existed in the early days with New Orleans music, each one of the lines of the instruments having its own function within the ensemble, playing separate lines. That's counterpoint. What we were doing was merely another application of the functions of the instrument.

"In Dixieland," he continued, "you had the clarinet riding on the top; the trumpet playing around the melody, establishing the lead line; and the trombone playing in an accompanying way, establishing the chord relationship that connects it with the rhythm section and with the trumpet/cornet line. Ours was different because it was a different kind of rhythmic approach. And the horns that we were relating were different. We didn't have the clarinet riding high. The trumpet was playing different kinds of melodies. I was still playing the harmony line, but the kinds of lines I was playing were structured differently. The rhythm was different. My whole job, when we left the piano off, was to establish always the sound of the chord progression that was moving through the piece," he said. Mulligan admitted that he sometimes had second thoughts about leaving out the piano. "In retrospect," he said, "I wish I had thought of having a piano in there. It would have taken a lot of the pressure off the rhythm section." That, of course, explains why he and Brookmeyer occasionally sat in at piano.

"The arrangements, by Mulligan, Bob Brookmeyer, and Al Cohn," Mark Gardner pointed out, "are wonderfully drawn: lush, yet transparent and not at all overblown." Gardner attributed this "in part, to the absence of a chordal instrument and, hence, of any of the incidental conflicts that normally occur in a big band when pianists or guitarists improvise harmonies while the reeds and brass play arranged harmonies."

"We had to start from the ground up putting a book together," Mulligan recalled. "I had Brookmeyer and Al Cohn working on charts, and I got [trumpeter Johnny] Carisi to write a couple of things that he had done.

Then, I brought in Bill Holman from California. Bill did the bulk of it. I wrote a couple of things, but I was making a big investment in this thing without any business managers or road managers or anything else." Johnny Mandel also wrote for the band. "Gerry had liked the things I'd written for *I Want to Live!*" Mandel said, "and asked me to do them for the Concert band. That Concert band was inspiring. It was unique. Gerry would write some of the things; Bobby would write some. Gerry didn't get to write as much as he would have liked, because he was so busy being a bandleader."

Mulligan acknowledged this in a 1960 interview with Nat Hentoff in the liner notes for the Verve album *Gerry Mulligan and the Concert Jazz Band at the Village Vanguard*. "So far as my own participation is concerned," he said, "my stamp is on the band, and I'm the featured soloist, but, up to now, I've been more of a supervisor of the writing than a very active contributor. But all of what we do is based on my conviction that music is to be *enjoyed*, by the player as well as the listener."

In 2011, the DIVA Jazz Orchestra, a fifteen-piece all-female big band, recorded an album on Arbors Records with Mandel called *Johnny Mandel: The Man and His Music*. DIVA's baritone saxophonist, Lisa Parrott, grew up in Australia and told me that one of her top-ten favorite records was "a used vinyl copy of the big band live at the Village Vanguard. It was such an amazing album. I listened to that to death." At the first rehearsal for the Mandel recording, she said, "the first tune was 'Black Nightgown' [from the *I Want to Live!* soundtrack and also on the *Village Vanguard* live recording]. I didn't realize that Johnny had written a lot of the arrangements for Gerry's big band. So, we're playing this chart, and I'm actually singing along with it. I think that record is still in my parents' garage, so I hadn't heard it in many, many years. But I knew exactly what was coming next. It was freaking me out. I felt incredibly honored that I got to play that and 'The Theme from *I Want to Live!*'"

The sound of the Concert Jazz Band, according to Bill Crow, "was a blending of all the different colors, like the weaving of a tapestry. The closest to it before was Claude Thornhill or some of the classical composers like Debussy and Ravel. I was pretty impressed by the Claude Thornhill band," he said, "even before they started doing the bebop things that Gil Evans wrote. When I went out to hear that band, I flipped out. I'd never heard a band sound like that."

Holman was "very flattered that Gerry asked me to help out. He'd been one of my big influences on the Kenton band," he told me. "I really jumped at the chance to be in New York for a while to be around all of these guys. It was a big deal for me. You could *feel* the guys on the bandstand. There was a lot of enthusiasm going on. We would look forward to the gigs; they weren't work sessions, they were treats. They'd talk about 'What can we do? How can we play this to make it sound better?' That was very rare among big bands. People have a lot of respect for that band. It will always be a lasting landmark."

Alan Raph was a twenty-seven-year-old, classically trained bass trombone player. He'd played in a couple of Broadway shows, had played first trombone with symphony orchestras, and had performed with Larry Elgart's jazz-oriented dance band. "I was walking the floor at the union one day," he told me, "and I saw Dick Hixon, who was another bass trombone player. He told me Gerry Mulligan was starting a band and that I ought to check it out. I got Gerry's number, called him up, and told him who I was. Mulligan asked, 'Where have you played?' I told him, and he said, 'But this is a jazz band.' He sounded annoyed, and I said, 'Well, I'm quick.' And he said, 'OK, come on down to rehearsal.'"

When Raph arrived at the rehearsal studio, on the second floor at 89th and Broadway, he looked around the room. "There's Brookmeyer and Zoot Sims, Dave Bailey (drums) and Bill Takas (bass). I sat down next to Brookmeyer, and the first tune was 'Walkin' Shoes.' I had the sense not to assert myself. I played exactly what Brookmeyer played. I tried to imitate him; I phrased the way he did. All I did was match my notes to his phrasing. I seemed to get by, so they called me for another rehearsal. I started rehearsing with the band, and that kind of put me aboard. At the time, Gerry Mulligan was a big, big name. I thought, 'Oh God, I'm playing with Gerry Mulligan.' I didn't realize the importance of the band outside of the fact that it was a band that Gerry Mulligan was leading."

The musicality between Mulligan and Brookmeyer, Raph said, "was impeccable." The playing of the ensemble, he added, "was pretty much the same every night, but the solos were different, they changed tremendously, and the backgrounds to the solos changed. Mulligan was pretty consistent. He would come in and play his thing, and it would always be interesting and very, very creative. It was the absolute highest level of jazz playing.

And Brookmeyer would come in on his solos, and I could never figure out where he was going to come from. He did 'Body and Soul' maybe one hundred fifty times with me sitting next to him, and I could never get a handle on where he was going to come in from. The two of them worked so well together."

The band's first tour was arranged by Norman Granz, who wanted to record the band for Verve. Granz, said Mulligan, "thought it was important to get the band together in this country, where people couldn't care less, before we took it to Europe where people were waiting. There was tremendous enthusiasm and excitement in Europe." According to Tad Hershorn, writing in *Norman Granz: The Man Who Used Jazz for Justice*, Granz ran a full-page ad in *Down Beat* in October 1960 publicizing the band's debut album, *Gerry Mulligan: The Concert Jazz Band*, as it began a multi-city U.S. tour before embarking for Western Europe.

"One of the things Norman wanted to do," Mulligan said, "was to record the band live, and he figured that certain halls would have recording equipment that could do that. So, the first place was the Santa Monica Civic Auditorium. We recorded at Santa Monica, as planned, went to Phoenix, and then to Hunter College in New York City. Our first dates in Europe were in Gothenburg and Stockholm in Sweden." *Gerry Mulligan and the Concert Jazz Band: Santa Monica 1960*, originally released by Granz's Verve label, was reissued in 2012 by Fresh Sound Records. "Gothenburg," Mulligan recalled, "was another place that Norman wanted to have a recording take place because he had the equipment, and they were going to do it in conjunction with a radio broadcast. Then we went on to Copenhagen and then to Berlin. Berlin was kind of a disaster because a couple of the guys got themselves into trouble. The next night we went to Paris; no recording but a radio broadcast, and the band was so tired. We wound up in Italy. It's amazing the album recorded in Europe sounds as cohesive as it does, because it was recorded in all different kinds of circumstances."

Mulligan was not always happy with the recorded versions of the band's live concerts. "I've always felt that in-person performances were totally different from a record. If you're sitting in a theater and a band does something, and they stretch out, and somebody takes another chorus, there's something physical that goes on; and the audience is with you. They can see it, and they understand why you're doing it. When you're listening [to a record], you don't necessarily have that same connection. And, musically, it may not make any sense at all. There are a lot of things about the interaction between an audience and the band when you're playing in front of them that is altogether different from the impact of the music when the physical element is not involved." As a result, Mulligan wanted to see some of the recordings edited down, but "Norman was a great believer in doing the things the way they were. He liked jam sessions for that reason. He thought a record should be a realistic presentation of what happened. I wanted to make a recording that people would want to play more than once."

Gardner felt the ensemble work "[rivaled] that of Basie's band of the 1950s." That achievement, he wrote, was "all the more amazing when one considers that these tunes were recorded in 'live' performance rather than in the studio. Here, in marked contrast to the monolithic, powerhouse playing of that Basie band, is a band that sings gorgeously and swings hard in a delicate and varied way."

A particularly memorable live appearance (along with a subsequent recording) of the band occurred on July 1, 1960, at the Newport Jazz Festival. The atmosphere is captured by writer Bill Milkowski on the Concert Vault website: "Performing before a crowd of 11,000 fans who stood patiently in the rain to dig his sounds, Mulligan delivered an exhilarating set that showcased valve trombonist Bob Brookmeyer, alto saxophonist Gene Quill, tenor saxophonist Jim Reider, trumpeter Don Ferrara, and the bandleader himself stretching out in the context of some well crafted tunes with ornate arrangements (by Bill Holman, Johnny Mandel, Al Cohn, Brookmeyer and Mulligan)." The concert encompassed a mix of Mulligan originals, including "Walkin' Shoes," standards such as "Broadway" (Billy Bird, Henry J. Wood, Teddy McRae), and Johnny Mandel's theme from *I Want to Live!* "Walkin' Shoes," according to Milkowski, was "another showcase for the bandleader's agile, melodic touch on the unwieldy bari sax against the tune's tightly woven horn arrangements." The theme from *I Want to Live!*, Milkowski wrote, "allows Mulligan to take his time and stretch out with his beautiful burnished tone on the bari, coloring the piece with his soulful, deep blue expression." The recording of that concert, *The Concert Jazz Band: At Newport 1960*, was digitally remastered and reissued in 2011 on the Ais label.

Raph remembered that the concert venue "was very crowded. We had a tent, and we had to change and warm up in the tent. It was full of photographers and people interviewing and all of that. At one point, Brookmeyer put a chair in the middle of the floor and got up on the chair and said, in a loud voice: 'Will you fucking people get out of here? We're trying to warm up and trying to do a concert, and you're in our faces, in our way. Just get the fuck out of here!'

"And that kind of set the mood. We went out and played, and that was it."

Gene Lees, who was the editor of *Down Beat*, recalled covering the concert in his book *Arranging the Score: Portraits of the Great Arrangers.* "I saw Gerry in person for the first time at the Newport Jazz Festival on the Fourth of July weekend of 1960," he wrote. "He had just organized what he called the Concert Jazz Band. In a flurry of publicity, it was to make its debut at Newport. The big band era was ended. Nobody—well, almost nobody—tried to launch big bands any more. The ballrooms and dance pavilions were gone or no longer booked bands . . . But I wanted to hear it: anything Mulligan did seemed likely to be innovative, as indeed that band was.

"I was backstage in a tent, talking with Dizzy Gillespie when the first sounds of the band came to us. It was raining torrents . . . The band began to perform Bob Brookmeyer's lyrical arrangement of Django Reinhardt's ballad 'Manoir de mes reves.' In front of the stage, rain danced on a garden of black umbrellas. An imaginative cameraman panned across this audience in the rain, then across the stage, coming to rest on a great puddle, in which an upside-down Mulligan was playing an exquisite obbligato to the chart, leading into his solo. I was watching both the image and the reality. It was one of the unforgettable musical moments of my life."

After the CJB made some of its first records, Brookmeyer and Mulligan decided they needed drummer Mel Lewis to be a permanent member of the band. "Mel was still on the staff at ABC in Hollywood," Mulligan recalled, "so we used to fly him back and forth until his staff job was over. Then he came east and joined the band full time." Bassist Bill Crow joined the band after it returned from its European tour. "When they came back to New York," Crow recalled, "the band had a West Coast rhythm section—Buddy Clark on bass and Mel Lewis on drums—and a West Coast hot trumpet player Conte Condoli. Mel decided to stay in New York, but Buddy and Conte went back to the West Coast. So there were two openings in the band, and it was coming into the Village Vanguard. Gerry called me and Clark Terry, and we joined the band when it couldn't have been hotter. It was at its peak. Clark stepped in with that huge bag of tricks that he had and just decorated the band so beautifully.

"With Clark in the trumpet section and Brookmeyer in the trombone section and Gerry in the saxophone section," Crow continued, "we could open up every chart we wanted to, and if somebody was playing a good solo, Gerry would go into the quartet mode. He'd start playing in backgrounds behind the solo like he did with the quartet, and the rest of the saxophone section would just harmonize what he was playing. And then Clark would think of something to answer it with the trumpets, and Bob would think of something to tuck the trombone section in; and we'd have a whole new head arrangement, and we wouldn't go with the rest of the written part until Gerry gave us the signal. So that meant that most of the rhythm tunes would stay alive and fresh every night, because they were never the same. And the band really understood how to do that. Everybody was a composer. It was really great."

Lewis told Hentoff, in the *Village Vanguard* liner notes, that, "Every time we play something, it's different from the last time we've played the number. That's the way it's supposed to be. This is a real jazz band."

Baritone saxophonist Gary Smulyan told me the *Village Vanguard* album is his favorite Gerry Mulligan record. "I think Gerry is very extroverted on that record," he said, "especially when he's trading with Clark Terry on the first piece. His humor comes out. He and Clark are trying to out quote each other and see how funny each one can be without cracking up." In the album's liner notes, Hentoff also commented on the rapport and humorous exchanges between Mulligan and Terry on the opening track, "Blueport," a composition by Art Farmer. "Bill Crow's bass solo," he wrote, "leads into a crackling series of exchanges between Gerry Mulligan and Clark Terry. Mulligan first takes the four-bar breaks with eight-bar answers from Terry. The process is then reversed. The dialogue is a contest of wit as well as quick-fingering imagination, and there are a couple of places where the two jousters nearly break each other up."

Raph knew Terry by reputation, but said, "I'd never played with him. As good as the band was—and the band was fantastically good—when Clark came in, the band shot up another 30 percent because of Clark.

He was so dynamic, and he was such a strong musical personality, that it became a better band. When Gerry played with Brookmeyer, they played off each other. When Gerry or Brookmeyer played with Clark, they also played off each other. But when it came Clark's turn to do his own contribution, he would go up to another level. It was always happy and positive and extremely creative. He could give to the situation, and then he could go beyond that for his own expression. He was truly incredible. There are certain people—when you mention them, the conversation stops. When you're talking about jazz trumpet and swinging and all of that, when you say 'Clark Terry,' the conversation stops."

Calling Terry "truly a player for all seasons," Raymond Horricks quoted the trumpeter in the October 11, 1998 issue of *Crescendo & Jazz Music* as saying that "Gerry's a real leader. He respects all the guys and knows how much they contribute, and you feel you're part of things."

New Yorker jazz writer Whitney Balliett recognized the presence of the quartet inside the big band. "One can hear the quartet playing hide-and-seek in almost every number," he wrote in the November 15, 1960 issue. "There are contrapuntal exercises between Mulligan and a trumpet or tenor saxophone or trombone."

The arrangement with Granz, Crow explained, would have "Norman picking up the losses in this country if he could keep the recordings, and then he could make some bread on the European tours. He had a band meeting and asked everyone to name the salary they could live with. Everybody kept their prices down as much as they could in order to keep that band hot. We couldn't believe how good the band was. We were at the Vanguard for a week. We'd get off the band at the end of a set, go into the kitchen and talk about the band, and couldn't wait to get back on. If somebody got a call for a record date, they'd turn it down because they didn't want to miss being there."

According to Hershorn, "The band's renown brought in a host of honors in 1960 and 1961 from the public and critics alike, including *Down Beat*'s annual international critics' poll and *Billboard*'s annual jazz writers' poll."

The reissue by Europe 1 of a live recording from Zurich, *Gerry Mulligan and the Concert Jazz Big Band feat. Zoot Sims: Zurich 1960,* inspired *Jazz Times* writer Doug Ramsey to assess the band's legacy in the September 2000 issue of that publication. "Night after night," Ramsey wrote, "during the short life of the Concert Jazz Band, Mulligan and his musicians imparted renewed freshness to its rich repertoire, from 'Walkin' Shoes' to Brookmeyer's imperishable arrangement of 'You Took Advantage of Me' to Johnny Mandel's 'Black Nightgown.' That is what happens when superb players under a gifted leader live with first-rate material long enough to absorb it and inhabit it. The band's recorded legacy is not in proportion to its importance."

Ramsey also saved some praise for Sims, calling his performance as guest soloist "a triumphal one . . . He played at a level of swing and invention seldom achieved by a soloist. Improvisation so exalted almost never takes place in a studio and is rarely captured on a live recording."

Granz impacted Mulligan's career in another way, quite apart from the Concert Jazz Band. Mulligan made a number of *Mulligan Meets* albums, facilitated by Granz. "I was lucky to have made contact with Norman Granz," he told *Down Beat*'s Michael Bourne in January 1989. "He knew the kinds of things I liked to do, and he liked to do those things, too. Norman came backstage at Newport a couple of years in a row, and he'd hear the conversation between Paul Desmond and me. Paul was always saying, 'We've got to record, do it like the quartet, only with the alto sax instead of the trumpet. I'll play Chet's part.' I'd say it was a great idea. Norman said, 'You guys are ridiculous. You'll talk about this for twenty years and never do it. Are you serious about doing it?' I said we were, and next thing we knew, Norman set up the studio."

Playing with Desmond, said *Jazz Review*'s Richard Cook, "Mulligan found a stylist whose sound and delivery dovetailed so handsomely with his own that the ongoing dialogue . . . is virtually seamless." Jerome Klinkowitz, in *Listen: Gerry Mulligan—An Aural Narrative in Jazz*, felt: "The vast differences in register and timbre between the alto and the bari are at once effaced by the two players' obvious enjoyment of each other's company . . . These two soloists build songs based on an awareness of each other's presence, interacting almost simultaneously rather than just interweaving lines . . ."

When Mulligan and Desmond's 1962 RCA Victor album *Two of a Mind* was reissued in 1989, the *Chicago Tribune*'s Jack Fuller, referring to them as "two of the smoothest, most lyrical sax players of their generation," in the

June 25, 1989 edition, said the rerelease was "like something new. The album was buried under the bossa-nova craze when it was first issued, but it has staying power. The duet improvisations, full of the Mulligan feeling for fugue, are delightful."

Other *Meets* collaborations were with Stan Getz, Johnny Hodges, Thelonius Monk, and Ben Webster. On the Getz album, he and Mulligan switched horns on one side.

In January 1961, Granz sold Verve to MGM and the financial arrangement with Mulligan disappeared. "Gerry had this payroll," Crow said, "and he didn't have anything booked until a month later in Boston. He said, 'I can't afford this band.' So he broke the band up." There continued to be concerts and recordings on a part-time basis, but Mulligan's primary activity was leading a quartet with Brookmeyer, Crow, and Lewis, Gus Johnson, or Dave Bailey on drums.

The Concert Jazz Band stayed together, off and on, until 1964, recording a total of five albums for Verve. According to Bill Kirchner in *The Complete Verve Gerry Mulligan Concert Jazz Band Sessions*, "All was not lost. The CJB still had two remarkable albums ahead: *A Concert in Jazz* and *Gerry Mulligan '63* . . . And it still played in public with a frequency that most part-time big bands today would envy." In fact, in a *Down Beat* review of the band's performance at Birdland in 1964, Ira Gitler wrote: "If this band cannot work when it wants to, there is something very wrong with the state of music in the United States." George T. Simon, in *The Big Bands*, called the Concert Jazz Band "one of the outstanding big bands of all time." Pointing out the influence of Claude Thornhill, Simon praised its "subtle, persuasive, swinging sounds. If ever there was classic proof that big band jazz needn't be loud or blatant to be effective, the Gerry Mulligan band was it."

The Concert Jazz Band, *Jazz Journal International*'s Ian Kendall wrote, was "a reminder of Mulligan's excellence as a composer/arranger/orchestrator—something that can be easily overlooked because of his obvious pre-eminence as a baritone saxophone player . . . It makes further use of the concept of the Miles Nonet. The establishment of the Band in 1960 as a working and recording unit was a clear demonstration of Mulligan's interest in obtaining flexibility and a variety of tone colours in a large ensemble."

In 2012, Fresh Sound Records reissued *Gerry Mulligan and the Concert Jazz Band: Santa Monica 1960.* The liner notes, written by producer Jordi Pujol, described the group as "the exciting Gerry Mulligan Concert Jazz Band that held the Santa Monica Civic Auditorium spellbound . . . By contemporary standards, this was a 'small' big band, made up of 13 men, performing according to Mulligan's very definite idea of how a band should work and sound. Though studded with stellar names, it was a close-knit team, with [tenor saxophonist] Zoot Sims as the featured guest soloist. There was room to stretch, but when the time came to get together, the boys were there." The twelve-page booklet that accompanied the album quoted Mulligan as saying: "My idea is not so much that we are a big band with a small-band feel, but that we have a big-band feel in the way that a big band ought to be."

In a 2002 review of the album for the website All About Jazz, Joel Roberts wrote that "What sets this ensemble apart isn't so much the compositions or even the star power of the soloists. The key is the cohesiveness of the band as a unit and the crisp, tight arrangements and orchestrations by Mulligan, Brookmeyer, and Al Cohn . . . Mulligan was no avant gardist, but he knew how to push the limits while working within a straight-ahead context, and he knew how to make a band swing."

When Mosaic Records reissued *The Complete Verve Gerry Mulligan Concert Band Sessions* in 2004, *Jazz Times*'s Nate Chinen wrote in April 2004 that "[the] remarkable flexibility of this large ensemble, and its blend of lightness and strength have few precursors." Lamenting the relative brevity of the band's existence, Chinen pointed out that, in his opinion, the Concert Jazz Band "set the stage for another ensemble: the eminent Thad Jones-Mel Lewis Orchestra. So, although short-lived, the Mulligan Concert Jazz Band had its lasting influence." And, the Mosaic reissue, he added, "should ensure that it has lasting documentation as well."

In 2006, saxophonist Ted Hogarth received his master's degree in jazz composition at DePaul University in Chicago. In celebration of this achievement, his wife, Lisa, gave him the complete four-disc Verve Concert Jazz Band recordings. "I had heard of Gerry because of the *Birth of the Cool* recordings when I was in high school in Michigan," Hogarth told me. "Other than that recording and some of the pianoless quartets he did with Chet Baker, I really hadn't explored a lot of his music."

The gift from his wife changed all that. "I had never heard the Concert Jazz Band before, and I just fell in love with it. Literally, for a year, all I listened to were those four discs. And it really changed my approach to sound on the saxophone. And all of a sudden, my focus on composition and arranging changed, because I had never heard an ensemble quite like this. I was taught how to write for traditional big bands, but then, hearing this smaller version just set me on fire, and it started a really cool journey."

That journey included the forming of the Mulligan Mosaic Band, based on the Concert Jazz Band's orchestration and arrangements. The band performs at clubs, concerts, festivals, and workshops in the Chicago area. Hogarth, at the time of our interview, was on the road touring with the pit orchestra of the Broadway show *Jersey Boys*, so the Mosaic band was on hiatus, but when he was last in Chicago, he said, "We did the Chicago Jazz Festival, a bunch of high school jazz festivals, and some educational outreach. It was amazing to me how many people knew of the Concert Jazz Band."

In the late 1970s, Mulligan surprised an audience at the Newport Jazz Festival in New York with a new version of the Concert Jazz Band. More on that later.

9

'I WAS THE SAXOPHONIST WHO CAME TO DINNER'

After the Concert Jazz Band broke up for good in 1964 and Judy Holliday died in 1965, Mulligan's musical activities were varied and somewhat unstructured. He made several albums on the Limelight label, a subsidiary of Mercury Records, and did a European tour with pianist Hampton Hawes. And he met actress Sandy Dennis.

Dennis, who died in 1992 at the age of fifty-four, won two Tony Awards, for *A Thousand Clowns* in 1963 and for her role in *Any Wednesday* in 1964. In 1966, she won an Academy Award for Best Supporting Actress in *Who's Afraid of Virginia Woolf.*

"I liked her a lot," Mulligan said, "and so we started going together. One thing that always stood out was the difference in personality between Sandy and Judy. Judy wanted to discuss things—everything needed to be out in the open with her. Sandy, on the other hand, was a very, very private person. It took me a long time to realize she never wanted to discuss things that had to do with her work, acting, the theater, the plays that she was doing. She was even reluctant to have me read for her. It was always peculiar to me, because I've always been very open about what I'm doing, what I'm thinking, the projects I'm working on, ideas I've got. Sandy was quite the opposite. I started early on to feel kind of shut out—she didn't particularly care or need anyone. So early on, we started to drift our own ways.

I started spending a lot of time in Europe. It was a kind of disorganized, unrewarding time for me." Despite this, they stayed together through the mid-1970s.

Musically, too, it was a somewhat perplexing time for Mulligan. Among the albums recorded for Limelight were *If You Can't Beat 'Em, Join 'Em* and *Feelin' Good*. In a review of *If You Can't Beat 'Em, Join 'Em*, on AllMusic, Ken Dryden pointed out that, in the early '60s, "Many jazz musicians were frustrated with the public's focus on rock & roll and pop music . . . So Mulligan, like many other jazzmen, decided to take a few of the hits and recast them in a jazz setting. Roger Miller's 'King of the Road' and 'Engine, Engine No. 9' retain their country flavor due to the presence of guitarist Johnny Gray, yet both tracks work because they are strong melodies on which Mulligan builds strong improvisations." The album also included jazz versions of songs by the Beatles, Petula Clark, and Bob Dylan.

If You Can't Beat 'Em, Join 'Em, Mulligan concluded, "was probably not a good idea. It kind of covered up what I was really doing and may have sounded like sour grapes. The idea of the album was quite simply to take the tunes and put them in our own setting. Some things came out very well, such as the version we do of 'Engine, Engine No. 9.' Pete Jolly plays such great choruses on the thing. You realize that the material has possibilities that aren't evident in the versions that everybody knows. The idea was to treat these pop tunes in the way we played, the way we thought, rather than where they came from."

Feelin' Good was recorded with a string section. The title tune was from the Anthony Newley–Leslie Bricusse Broadway musical *The Roar of the Greasepaint – The Smell of the Crowd*. Other tracks included such selections as the Sammy Cahn–Jimmy Van Heusen standard "The Second Time Around" and "The Shadow of Your Smile," written by Johnny Mandel and Paul Francis Webster for the soundtrack to the movie *The Sandpiper*. Mulligan hired New Zealander Julian Lee to write the arrangements. "Julian Lee," he said, "was a very talented guy. I thought his writing for a small string section was terrific. They were very effective, simple arrangements. We recorded the tracks first, knowing that Julian was going to add string parts to it. I loved the way it came out, some really beautiful stuff in there."

Reached at his home in New South Wales Australia, the ninety-year-old Lee said it was "a big thrill to have the pleasure of working with Gerry Mulligan because I've always been a great admirer of his. He was very meticulous about how he wanted things done. I spent quite a lot of time with him, discussing the tracks we were going to do." One aspect of the album Lee particularly liked was that Mulligan "played a lot of clarinet. He loved to play the clarinet. He thoroughly enjoyed doing that."

Blind from birth, Lee spent fourteen years in California after having been a bandleader and arranger for the New Zealand Broadcasting Service and an arranger for the Australian Broadcasting Service. "I did quite a lot of arrangements for other people," he recalled. "I did two albums for the Three Sounds, five albums for George Shearing, and I did quite a lot of commercial albums with people like Vicki Carr."

Feelin' Good, available today only on vinyl, received a positive review from Dryden. "Although the presence of a 10-piece string section conducted and arranged by Julian Lee might make some jazz fans assume this Gerry Mulligan date borders on easy listening," he wrote on AllMusic, "that's hardly the case. The strings are used judiciously for color instead of overwhelming the music, while most of the tracks are either classic ballads or overlooked gems . . . the focus is on the leader's warm, melodic solos. While this long unavailable LP obviously can't be considered among the top tier of his recordings, Mulligan fans will not be disappointed if they can locate copies."

Still, Mulligan felt that the period was "a fairly unrewarding time for me. I did a tour for some weeks with Hampton Hawes, and I enjoyed playing with him, but I really didn't enjoy knocking around Europe very much. I was used to having my own band and playing what I want, but the last thing I did with my own quartet was in '64. I was playing mostly with European rhythm sections."

The '60s represented an unhappy period for Mulligan for another reason. A white musician who had been accepted by black musicians such as Ben Webster and Miles Davis, he felt that during the '60s, "younger black musicians had a chip on their shoulders. They felt 'whitey' had stolen their music. There was a cutting off of communication between people who should have been in communication with each other. The resentments and negativism was destructive. That went on in the '60s, and I guess it was even worse in the '70s."

That contrasted with his early years in New York. "I was very much accepted by the other musicians," he said. "Many were my own age, and many were older. Through the '40s and when I had my own group in the '50s, there was never a distance created by racial attitudes. The thing that was going on in jazz was quite different from what was going on in the real world. Jazz was in the forefront of trying to get people together. It was at the forefront of having blacks and whites work together in bands. Even before they were working together, in the '20s and '30s, black arrangers were arranging for white bands and white arrangers were arranging for black bands."

The "abrupt change" in attitude among some of the black musicians confused and hurt Mulligan. "A lot of black musicians," he said, "were angry. It was as if we'd chosen up sides. It was amazing to me that they had this division in their heads that we (white musicians) were the enemy.

"I didn't grow up being aware of any tensions," he continued. "Lily"—the African-American woman who assisted his mother—"was my touchstone with reality. I was naive enough so I could accept life the way it was. The black guys were friends with the white guys, and we worked together. When I was in high school and hanging out backstage at various places, one of the guys who befriended me was Trummy Young." Young was a trombonist about fifteen years older than Mulligan who played with Earl Hines, Jimmie Lunceford, and Charlie Barnet, among others. "He was a great guy. He and a few other musicians just liked having a kid around who was enthusiastic about music."

Nothing epitomized this attitude better than the CBS television special *The Sound of Jazz*, which aired on December 6, 1957. Mulligan was one of a few white musicians playing with such giants as Count Basie, Thelonius Monk, Coleman Hawkins, and Ben Webster. As noted, he also played the first solo behind Billie Holiday's performance of "Fine and Mellow." Other solos behind Holiday were played by Webster and Lester Young. Mulligan remembered that the program was aired from "this big studio on New York's 11th Avenue. They had the Basie band set up on one side of the room, and they had a small band setup for Thelonius Monk over in this corner and, halfway down the hall, it was set up for Pee Wee Russell and Jimmy Giuffre. On the opposite corner was a setup for all of the horns in a semicircle behind Billie. The whole focus was the music, and everybody else stayed as much as they could out of the way so there was this focus of all the musicians on each other. There were some warm moments and some funny moments. At one point in Monk's set, Monk was playing some kind of angular squawky thing and the camera goes to Count Basie's face. Count is sitting there smiling, kind of nodding his head. Everybody involved who loved this music would say, 'Why don't they use that as a model and do it again?' But nobody ever wanted to do it again. They didn't know what they had done."

According to Geoffrey Ward and Ken Burns in *Jazz: A History of America's Music*, *The Sound of Jazz* "remains the high-water mark of jazz on American television." In 1959, Robert Herridge, the producer of *The Sound of Jazz*, produced another jazz program on CBS as part of his *Robert Herridge Theater*. Airing on April 2, 1959, it featured a quintet with Miles Davis on trumpet, John Coltrane on tenor saxophone, Wynton Kelly on piano, Paul Chambers on bass, and Jimmy Cobb on drums.

Freelancing with European rhythm sections came to an end for Mulligan in 1968, when George Wein brought Dave Brubeck and Mulligan together. Brubeck had broken up his quartet when alto saxophonist Paul Desmond left the group. "I remember talking to Dave," Wein told me, "and I remember talking to Gerry. And I said, 'Why don't you guys get together?' It was a natural. Gerry did not have his own group, and Desmond had left Brubeck."

"George Wein had a date he wanted us to play," Mulligan recalled. "It was a festival in New Orleans. Dave was getting a rhythm section together—Jack Six on bass and Alan Dawson on drums. So, I went down to New Orleans and played that thing with them. Then some other dates came up because we had done that together. We recorded an album in Mexico City called *Compadres*. So for the next few years, most of the stuff I did was with Dave. That gave me a rest from being a bandleader." Speaking to Brubeck in the video *Listen: Gerry Mulligan*, Mulligan said, "I was the saxophone player who came to dinner. It was great for me because, after all those years of being the leader and having to worry about getting the [airline] tickets, it was great. You just aimed me in the right direction, and I was there."

The period with Brubeck, Wein told me, was a good respite from band leading for Mulligan. "If Gerry was coming to play with other people,"

Wein said, "he would be having a ball. But when he had his own band and had to perform, he became a different person. He was so tense. He wanted everything to be so correct. And it was so difficult. He was a perfectionist with his own group—not just with the music, but with every single thing about it." Loras Schissel, an acquisitions specialist in the music division at the Library of Congress, believes there was a part of Mulligan that preferred just to be a player. "He always said," Schissel recalled, "how much he liked to sit in with a band and just be the bari player."

The chemistry between Brubeck and Mulligan was natural. In the liner notes for *The Last Set at Newport*, an album featuring the Dave Brubeck Quartet, Bill Milkowski described that July 5, 1969, Newport performance. "'This Saturday evening engagement," he wrote, "found Brubeck, Mulligan, and the regal rhythm tandem of bassist Six and drummer Dawson to be truly on one accord in a stellar performance that wowed the Newport faithful at Freebody Park. They open with a soulful loping blues which eventually morphs into the Duke Ellington staple, 'Things Ain't What They Used to Be.' From the outset, Mulligan is in a laid-back mood on top of Dawson's loose, interactive swing pulse. Brubeck comps forcefully behind Mulligan's solo before launching into a harmonically provocative solo of his own that introduces some edgier elements into the proceedings while still remaining true to the spirit of Ellingtonia."

Another significant album made during the Brubeck-Mulligan period was *Live at the Berlin Philharmonic*, which was reissued as a two-disc set in 1995 by Sony. Bassist Jack Six told me the venue was extremely frenzied. "It was set up to be a television show. There were cameras and mikes all over the place," he said. "All of a sudden, Gerry's playing as a soloist, and they've got cameras in his face, so it got to a point where he was turning his back and walking around the stage. He kept doing that, and the audience started whistling, which was a sound of disapproval. I don't remember how they resolved it."

Despite the chaos, the resulting recording was a success. "Not only are the musicians in top form," wrote Scott Yanow on AllMusic, "but the audience is very enthusiastic, demanding three encores."

The rapport and creativity shared by Brubeck and Mulligan was described by Iola Brubeck in an interview in the *Listen: Gerry Mulligan* video. "Gerry and Dave did this duet one night," she said, "and what was interesting to me was, they chose the same tune every night—'These Foolish Things.' But every night it was absolutely different. There were times when it was very lyrical, somewhat sad, maybe soulful. And then maybe the next night, it would be bright and full of humor. I wish we had a recording of each night because you would have umpteen different variations of the mood of 'These Foolish Things.' It was never the same." Dave Brubeck characterized Mulligan this way: "If something hit him that inspired him, you couldn't hold him back. He'd jump in. In the middle of my chorus, he'd be buzzing like a wild bumblebee. Whatever was going on, he wanted to be part of it. He didn't like standing around waiting his turn. He'd jump in and try to make more happen, and he did."

Playing with Brubeck sparked Mulligan's interest in combining jazz with classical music. "Dave had done a lot of stuff for symphony at that point," he said. "He did a lot of stuff with orchestras and chorus. I was lucky that the period I was playing with him, he was doing some stuff with the Cincinnati Symphony. That was the first experience I had with a symphony. He wrote a couple of sections that were especially for me to play. And I really enjoyed it, so I started thinking at that point, 'Where can I get material to play with an orchestra?' That's the hardest thing to really conceive of. It's not just a question of putting a jazz musician with an orchestra. The material they're going to do together has to mean something to both sides. You can't just have the orchestra there providing cushions for soloists. If you adapt the jazz soloists to the orchestra, then you lose the jazz element. But that started me trying to come up with some sort of repertoire to play concerts with an orchestra."

In the early '70s, Mulligan got the itch to form his own band again, and he put together a sextet with a rhythm section that was the antithesis of the pianoless quartet—piano, guitar, bass, drums, and percussion. That was the genesis of a new big band that recorded *The Age of Steam* on A&M Records, an album that represented a departure from Mulligan's previous work and, in his words, "a turning point.

"A young fellow, a friend of [pianist] Roger Kellaway, wanted me to do an album for A&M. He was producing things for Herb Alpert," Mulligan said. Alpert, a trumpet player, had cofounded A&M in 1962 with a partner, Jerry Moss. It is generally considered one of the industry's most successful independent record labels. "I holed myself up at the Beverly

Wilshire Hotel," Mulligan said, "and got a piano brought in. When I had the stuff written—out of that came *The Age of Steam*. It was kind of an interesting instrumentation. The material I wrote could be performed in different ways. We had a five-piece rhythm section, four horns [on the] front line, and then there was an ensemble to back it up—a couple more trumpets, a couple more trombones. It added up to a good-size band—six brasses, five saxes, something like that. It was flexible. I did a couple of concerts with the full band, and I did things with just the four horns. And I started this new sextet that was based on the rhythm section and the one horn. *The Age of Steam* did work, and I always liked the album very much. Harry Edison [trumpet] was on it and Tom Scott [tenor sax] and Roger Kellaway, Howard Roberts on guitar, Brookmeyer, Bud Shank [alto sax], Jimmy Cleveland [trombone], Ernie Watts [tenor sax]. I did most of the writing in a week or ten days, and we wound up with more than enough material."

Other musicians on the album included trumpeter Roger Bobo, bass trombonist Ken Shroyer, bassist Chuck Domanico, drummer John Guerin, percussionist/drummer Joe Porcaro, and vibraphonist/percussionist Emil Richards. The solos were taken by Mulligan, Scott, Shank, Brookmeyer, and Edison. The album contains eight tracks, all Mulligan compositions. The best-known composition from the album was probably "K-4 Pacific," inspired by Mulligan's attraction to trains. "I was fascinated by trains as a kid," he told Michael Cuscuna, the record producer who wrote the original liner notes. "The sound of that locomotive made a large impression on me," he continued, "so I wrote this jazz chart with that sound and feeling in mind." Kellaway, in a separate video interview released with *Listen: Gerry Mulligan*, said, "One of the things that endears me to that particular album is Gerry's love for trains, because I have always loved trains."

Other compositions included "Golden Notebooks," which Cuscuna said was taken from the title of a Doris Lessing novel "in which an emotionally hung-up American [male] writer takes a prized golden notebook from the heroine, a really terrific English girl—also a writer. It is symbolic of all that he has taken from her already. Gerry wrote this piece to acknowledge all of the tangible and intangible things that men in our society steal from women."

"Maytag," according to Cuscuna, is a piece that "draws on Gerry's childhood experiences in his mother's basement with that soulful Maytag washer just chugging away with its own special rhythm."

Raymond Horricks, writing in the February 3, 1998, issue of *Crescendo & Jazz Music*, said *The Age of Steam* "was not only a watershed recording for Mulligan, but I would place it among the twenty best jazz recordings I've ever heard." Horricks singled out Mulligan's "getting together with electrified keyboards . . . The high quality of the solos. And his picking up on some younger jazz 'fusion' players like saxist Tom Scott. But *movement* comes out tops: in every demonstrable way."

Mulligan further explained his philosophy with regard to *The Age of Steam* in an interview with *Down Beat*'s Patricia Willard in the October 24, 1974 issue. "I use both electric piano and Fender [Rhodes] bass," he told her, "but I don't think they are substitutes for acoustic piano and bass. I like using them for certain sounds and rhythmic feelings because they are different, but I would gladly give up the luxury of electronics if I had to make a choice. I could never live exclusively with amplified instruments."

He continued to clarify his use of electronic instruments in a July 15, 1976 *Down Beat* interview with Arnold Jay Smith. "The instruments themselves," he said, "are made for particular orchestrations. They are not substitutes for the acoustic instruments. But there is plenty of room in a rhythm section for both kinds of sounds."

Kellaway pointed out that the rhythm section, plus Tom Scott on tenor, was really the Roger Kellaway Quartet or the Tom Scott Quartet. "At the time, we were two quartets, depending upon who got the gig. So *The Age of Steam* had that as its nucleus. And Emil Richards on percussion was part of my cello quartet.

"The track I like the best on the album is 'Grand Tour.' It's a beautiful ballad, so simple and poignant. One of the things Gerry always had was a gift for melody. That is one of the hardest things to do—to write a beautiful ballad, to play a beautiful ballad solo that's really meaningful."

Recording *The Age of Steam* was for Kellaway an extremely enjoyable—if not necessarily unique—experience. "Many of the experiences you have in the studio," he explained, "are ones of social engagement. When you walk in and you see old friends, and you know you're going to have a good time, because you enjoy hanging out with these people and playing with these people. We were hanging out and having some fun. I was happy to be with Gerry and to be able to support Gerry."

Tom Scott was thrilled to be on the album. "Gerry Mulligan had been a hero of mine since the age of ten," he said, also in a separate video interview released with *Listen: Gerry Mulligan*. "And I got to play with Bob Brookmeyer as well. Bob Brookmeyer and Gerry Mulligan were masters of a kind of playing that is not that common anymore. They were always playing contrapuntally, a wonderful kind of ESP going on. The horns were set up in a row. Brookmeyer was on one side of me, Mulligan on the other. It was like listening to Bach duets, listening to these two guys improvise around each other. There were sections that were written out, but there would be areas where it was very loose. It was very inspiring."

Mulligan pointed out to *Down Beat*'s Joe Klee in the May 29, 1974 issue that there were "really three stages to the *Age of Steam* band. This [sextet that Klee was reviewing at New York's Half Note club] is the basic rhythm quintet. Another stage adds trombone and soprano sax and sometimes trumpet to the front line. Then there is the full sized big band, heard at Newport last summer [and appearing on the album]."

The Age of Steam, Mulligan felt, was sort of like a crossroads because "It really kind of recharged my batteries. I had been in the doldrums and really depressed and down. It got me enthusiastic again. After that, I started another group based on the rhythm section of *The Age of Steam.* I had Bob Rosengarden on drums, George Duvivier on bass, Dave Samuels on vibes/percussion, a guitar player named Mike Santiago, and Tom Fay on piano." Duvivier, Mulligan said, "was a wonderful player and a funny man." Samuels, he added, liked to play vibes more than percussion, and "he always added something nice to the arrangements." Fay had already done some arranging for Mulligan. "That was a nice band," Mulligan said, "and we had that together for a couple of years. I essentially kept that instrumentation for a while."

Joe Lang, a columnist for *Jersey Jazz* magazine, caught the *Age of Steam* band on a night in the early '70s when Hank Jones subbed for Roger Kellaway. Writing in March 1996, Lang recalled the experience at the uptown Half Note Club and "enjoying for perhaps the only time I can remember the integration of some elements of rock into a jazz group. I could not believe that an electric piano could sound as good as Hank Jones made it sound that evening."

The spirit of the sextet was later captured by John Wilson of *The New York Times*. In a February 28, 1975 review of the group's performance at Hopper's in Greenwich Village, Wilson wrote, "The group is a reflection of Mr. Mulligan's personality—relaxed, slyly humorous, but, in performance, totally involved. It is a refreshing and provocative addition to jazz."

10

'YOU WANT ME TO BE THE MAGIC FLUTE PLAYER?'

Once the spark about combining jazz and classical music had been lit during the Brubeck years, Mulligan was enticed by the possibilities. He commissioned Frank Proto, a composer and bassist with the Cincinnati Symphony, to write something for him. "He wrote something he called a concerto," Mulligan said, "but I'm not sure it was strictly a concerto. It was relatively successful. We performed it a couple of times, but it pointed up the difficulties as much as it made use of the possibilities.

"If you were going to have improvisation with the orchestra, how do you go about it? This was always a problem, even with jazz writers. Composers who write for the symphony are not really aware that it's a special kind of an approach to write a successful chord progression for an improviser. Symphony writers frequently fall into the same trap. They'll write a complicated chord progression that really doesn't relate to a songlike melody. It's like a series of chords that are not really a progression. As a consequence, it throws a tremendous load on the soloist to make some kind of a structure over this progression that adds up to music.

"It happens a lot. It even happened in the piece [jazz arranger] Eddie Sauter wrote called *Focus* that Stan Getz recorded. Stan did a hell of a job improvising on this, but Eddie never gave him a place to settle." (*Focus* was an album originally released in 1961 by Verve and reissued in 1997 by

Polygram Records. Getz had commissioned Sauter to write some classical compositions for him to improvise on. Getz reportedly listened to the compositions once and then played tenor saxophone solos over them.)

In 1974, Mulligan traveled to Italy to make an album with Astor Piazzolla, an Argentinian composer known for injecting classical and jazz elements into his tango compositions. "He had made a new idiom out of the tango," Mulligan said, "and it turned out he had a fantasy of doing an album with me, dating from the *Birth of the Cool* and my pianoless-quartet days. So there were these Italian guys who commissioned him to do this album. He wrote all this music, and I wrote one piece. Astor wrote an arrangement of my piece, kind of a tango instrumentation that he had devised. He played an instrument called the *bandoneon*; it was like the grandfather of the accordion, a big powerful instrument with no keyboard on it—all buttons. Watching him play was incredible, very modern voicings on the thing. To reach the buttons, his fingers looked like snakes. It really had an uncanny sense to it. He was triple-jointed in his fingers."

Contessa Franca Rota had met Piazzolla and his wife and invited them to her house on the Adriatic coast during the summer of '74 to work on the album with Mulligan. "I had an apartment in Rome and a villa in Le Marche which belonged to my first husband," she told me. "At that time, I was going through a separation, but the family let me use the villa for a while. In my apartment in Rome, I had lots of artists as guests, and one of them brought Astor Piazzolla." Piazzolla told Franca that his wife was coming to Italy, "'and I don't know where to go this summer to write for this album for Gerry Mulligan. It's the dream of my life.'" Franca had no idea who Gerry Mulligan was, but her friend Clarissa Vallmitjana, who was her guest for the summer, suggested she invite Piazzolla and his wife to spend the summer with them. "I was kind of down about the whole story with my nearly ex-husband, so I invited him. He came to Le Marche with his wife. It was incredible to see him writing and so enthusiastic. Then he said, 'I'm going to leave for Milano, where I'm going to record it. Please come.'"

The recording date in Milan took place in September. The resulting album, *Summit*, was originally released on the Italian label Erre T.V. In 1990, it was released in the U.S. on the Ans Record label as *Summit – Reunion Cumbre*. In a review that now appears on AllMusic, John Storm Roberts described it as "mostly dark and moody music, with a lot of tonal variety and a resolute refusal to fit into any of the handy pigeonholes: a one-off event, wholly successful." Seven of the eight tracks were Piazzolla compositions. One track, "Aire de Buenos Aires," was a Mulligan composition.

"I was recording with Astor," Mulligan said, "and one day Franca came into the studio. I look up in the control room at one point, and I nudged Astor and said, 'Who's that beautiful girl in there? Who is she?' He said, 'Oh, it's just a girl.' So, we're listening back to the thing we had just recorded, and he introduced me to her. After a while, I look up, and she'd left. I was really kind of teed off at Astor."

According to Franca, Piazzolla had said, "If you don't come to the recording, I'll never talk to you." "I went there, and there was Gerry, this very charismatic and handsome fellow with long hair and a big saxophone, playing 'Aire de Buenos Aires,' the song that he wrote. It was wonderful." She remembers Piazzolla and Mulligan inviting her for dinner, but "I said, 'No, thank you,' because I already [had] another engagement." The friends with whom Franca had dinner plans were apparently astounded that she turned down the dinner invitation, saying, "You didn't go to dinner with Gerry Mulligan? You're crazy." Franca, describing Mulligan as "a fantastic player," added that he was "a wonderful person to look at."

The recording was finished two days later, and Mulligan recalled that "Astor was busy that night. His wife, Annalisa, had come, so they went off somewhere. I went off with the other guys. There were only one or two restaurants open late in Milan. So we went to this place called Santa Lucia. We get to the entrance of the place and start to go in, and I look across the room, and I see Franca sitting there with another woman. So I kind of push our whole party in the direction toward the table and sit down next to Franca. What I didn't know was that the woman she was sitting with was her sister-in-law, wife of her brother, and they were in the midst of a project. Her sister-in-law, Yolaine, had designed a line of clothes for children, and they were photographing the clothes for *Harper's Bazaar*, for what they called the *Baby Bazaar*. Franca was the photographer, so during the course of the dinner, Yolaine asked Franca, 'Why don't you ask him to come out and pose with the children?'"

Franca asked him if he'd like to come to the photo shoot and have his picture taken with some children for the baby fashions. Mulligan remembered saying, "Of course." Franca remembers that he actually said, "Oh, you want me to be the magic flute player?"

"It was ten o'clock on a Sunday morning, just what I was dying to do," Mulligan said. "Next morning, while they were getting dressed, I started noodling around on the saxophone, and Franca took a picture which turned out really well. Then, we spent the morning and afternoon doing stuff with the children."

"He took out his mouthpiece," Franca recalled, "and I started taking pictures then. We went to the park, and I took more pictures. It *was* like a magic flute, with the kids behind him. He asked me to go out to dinner, and I said I was too exhausted."

Mulligan left for Rome the next morning, and Franca took the photographs to *Harper's Bazaar*. "They said, 'You're having here a scoop. You have to interview him. Here's a ticket. You have to go to Rome and interview him immediately.' I flew to Rome, and we had dinner together. The next morning he asked me to have breakfast with him. He left for the airport to go to New York. The next day I go to Milano, and I give the article to *Harper's Bazaar*.

"Every night I was out for dinner, and every night he was able to reach me at dinnertime at the places where I was. It was so amazing because these people were not even listed. After five or six days like that, it was eleven o'clock at night, and I was at my friends' house for dinner, and the phone rings. 'Do you love me?' he asked. 'What about breakfast tomorrow morning?' I look at my watch, and I think, 'He'll never make it.' So I say, 'Why not?' The next morning, the bell of the apartment rings, and it's Gerry. 'We are supposed to have breakfast together,' he said. He took my hand, and from then on, we were always together. I never asked him how he found me every night. I thought it was very magic, very mysterious. I like to keep it that way."

Mulligan had to return to the U.S. because the UAB production of *Happy Birthday* was going to be presented in December. He invited Franca to join him in Birmingham. "I found out she was going to Venezuela to visit with some friends," Mulligan said, "so I decided to go to Birmingham by way of Venezuela. She came to Birmingham a few days later when she left Venezuela and said she'd do the cooking if she didn't have to do any cleaning up." The production, starring

Fannie Flagg, ran for about a week, and Mulligan thought that "with a hip director and someone working on jokes to bring them up to date, it probably could have been improved for Broadway purposes. It's too bad there was nobody connected with it who could push it in a way that it could even have been done in regional theater or dinner theater. That turned out to be the only time we ever did it." Franca's presence, though, helped. "Franca brought a kind of spirit to the thing," he said, "because the musicians really liked her. The girl that was playing the tenor and flute was kind of shy, and Franca made an atmosphere that kind of got everyone warmed up."

Saxophonist Ted Nash, who would later play in the new Concert Jazz Band that formed in 1978, remembered that "Franca used to lecture us on how we ate food. When we were in Connecticut, she would serve all the food, and we would go for the salad first. She would say, 'You don't eat the salad first; you eat it after.'" Franca also recalled some of those culinary moments. "Traveling, the musicians were introduced to very different places," she said. "I didn't want them to be criticized. They didn't know how to eat pasta, which is not easy. I showed them how to roll the pasta. It was very funny because the spaghetti was flying everywhere. We had a very good time. I enjoyed their personalities."

Before the Venezuela trip, Mulligan had to stop in New York for a reunion concert with Chet Baker, which resulted in a 1975 recording on the CTI label, *Carnegie Hall Concert*. Mulligan and Baker were backed by a contemporary rhythm section consisting of Bob James on keyboards, Ron Carter on bass, Harvey Mason on drums, Dave Samuels on vibraphone, and John Scofield on guitar. In a review on AllMusic, Scott Yanow reported that "some of the old magic was still there between the horns and, in addition to two of Mulligan's newer tunes, this set also includes fresh versions of 'Line for Lyons' and 'My Funny Valentine.'" The album (the first of two volumes) included four Mulligan compositions in addition to "Line for Lyons," "For an Unfinished Woman," "Song for Strayhorn," "It's Sandy at the Beach," and "K-4 Pacific."

Jack Chambers, reviewing the album for *Coda* in September 1976, wrote that "Mulligan's playing is superb, as if he was turned on by the reunion. He swings hard as always, but here his phrases have an uncommon bite." Chambers described Baker's playing as "diffident, and it is hard to tell if his playing will get a response from new listeners, but it will certainly touch those who can remember the better days."

Guitarist Scofield is still amazed that he was part of that band and the subsequent recording. "I was living in Boston," he told me. "I had attended Berklee, but I had dropped out and was just working around town, trying to get into the jazz scene. Gerry came to town to play at the Jazz Workshop for a week, and he wanted to add vibes and guitar to his quartet, so he called Alan Dawson, the drummer." Dawson, who spent time as Dave Brubeck's drummer, was teaching at Berklee. "Alan recommended me and Dave Samuels," Scofield continued, "so we played a week with Gerry's group with Bill Goodwin on drums, Jack Six on bass, and Tom Fay on piano. It was great. We got to hang with Gerry and meet him. I couldn't believe I was playing with a jazz legend."

The next gig with Mulligan for Scofield and Samuels was the Chet Baker reunion at Carnegie Hall. That, said Scofield, "was unbelievable. We didn't know he was going to call back for anything. Gerry wanted to use his working quartet for the concert, but [CTI Records founder] Creed Taylor wouldn't go for that rhythm section. But Gerry was somehow able to get us on the gig. We were unknown. When I go back and listen," Scofield said, "I realize what an amateur I was and what a pro Gerry was. And Chet, on the Carnegie Hall stuff, sounds incredible. It was just great to be there."

Franca recalled that "Gerry had told me the story of how Chet Baker kind of conned him, and how he went to jail and Chet Baker didn't. The only way Chet Baker could come back to play and to be hired to play, after being in drug rehabilitation and things like that, would be if he could do the reunion to reestablish his reputation as a good player. And Gerry said yes, he would do it. I wasn't there for the concert or the album, but I went there when they rehearsed. Gerry was gentle and kind. That was what I always admired—the kindness and generosity of this man. No resentment. Gerry had an ego, but a very good ego, not a selfish one. He had a temper because he was very tough with people when they were not giving the maximum they could give."

Bassist Ron Carter did recall some friction between Mulligan and Baker at rehearsal, but also had to leave the rehearsal early, due to another commitment. The ensuing concert, he said, "was good. It was fun. I just had to play like Bill Crow, so Gerry could play those contrapuntal lines. It was a very successful musical concert."

After the Venezuela trip, Mulligan and Franca returned to New York together. "It was nearly Christmastime," Franca remembered. "When I first met Gerry, it was October. So, he said, 'Now, we go to my home in Westport, Connecticut.' I said, 'I know you're separated, but you're still living with your kind-of friend—Sandy Dennis.' He said, 'No, no, I'll call her up.' He called her up, and he said she was delighted. I thought to myself, 'These Americans are very strange, but they're good friends, and that's fine.' So we went to Westport, and that night she was performing in New York, so we waited for her to have dinner. Gerry said, 'Why don't we prepare something?' and I said, 'It's your home. You prepare something.' So, Gerry's preparing the sauce or something, and she comes in, and she sees him cooking, and she looks at me, and she went ape. She lost her temper. I said to Gerry, 'We leave the house immediately,' but he said there was nothing open in Westport. So the next morning, I went to buy her a book on cats, thanked her for her hospitality—and out!" (Dennis, a known cat lover, once told *People* magazine, "If I didn't have these thirty-seven cats and three dogs, I think I would have been compulsive.")

Franca returned to Italy in early 1975, coming back to the New York area in the spring, when Mulligan was touring with his quartet. They rented a cottage together in Rowayton, Connecticut, bought a house in Darien, Connecticut, in 1979, and got married on June 5, 1982.

11

'ONE OF THE MOST IMPORTANT ARRANGERS IN THE HISTORY OF MUSIC'

From the mid-'70s until the time of his death in 1996, Mulligan's performances varied a great deal, ranging from regular appearances with his quartet and big band to guest spots with symphony orchestras to special duo performances with other jazz musicians such as pianist Billy Taylor and tenor saxophonist Scott Hamilton. He also spent a great deal of time composing and arranging, often in Italy.

Bassist Frank Luther joined Mulligan's quartet in early 1974, a relationship that would last, off and on, for about ten years. "I played with four different piano players and four different drummers," Luther told me. "I had come to New York from Chicago, and as soon as I got to the city, I just went out to clubs and sat in." Luther was introduced to Mulligan by vibraphonist-mellophonist Don Elliott. "It was interesting that he hired me," Luther reflected. "I was a raw talent because I was self-taught, but I guess Gerry saw the potential in me. He became my mentor, even though at times, he called me his nemesis.

"One of the things I learned was that Gerry liked control; he also liked to give you freedom—but not to the point where it sounded like mutiny. That was the fine line. If his energy level was up, you could go to that fine line and beyond it; and he was with you. But if his energy level was low, the paranoid thing would happen: 'Are these guys trying to take over the ship?' So, it was that kind of didactic. One night he would come up to me and say, 'I loved what you did tonight.' But, at the next concert, he would ask, 'Why didn't you do this?'"

Luther recalled a 1984 concert at Carnegie Hall where bands led by Mulligan and Lionel Hampton were playing with the New York Pops. "The New York Pops had one bassist who was a jazz player, and he was sick. So the contractor came up to me and said, 'The bass player's sick. Can you do this concert with Lionel Hampton?' I had never played with Lionel Hampton before, but Hampton and I connected. At the end of the concert, we're upstairs, and Lionel Hampton goes up to Gerry and says, 'This bass player you got, he's great!' And Gerry says, 'Yeah, that was tonight.'"

One of Luther's last gigs with Mulligan was in Connecticut at an outdoor concert. "We're playing a tune, and he gives me a solo," Luther said. "And I took three choruses. He comes up to me as I'm finishing the third chorus and says, 'Is it OK if I play?' So, the next tune, he gives me a solo, and I decide I'm just going to do two choruses. He says to me, 'Take another one.' It was that kind of relationship, but I really looked up to him. When you're in the middle of it, when it's happening, you don't really appreciate it. I appreciate it now. I wish I could play with Gerry now. There were really magical moments that he and I had together. I'm ready to play with him now."

That's a sentiment that is shared by other former Mulligan sidemen. "I only wish he were alive today," said drummer Rich DeRosa, "because when you're twenty-four years old, you don't have enough perspective. We knew he was a jazz legend, but you didn't really appreciate the valuable lessons you were learning at the time."

Pianist Bill Charlap, who has led his own trio since 1997 and is considered one of the leading jazz interpreters of the American popular songbook, was just starting out when he played with Mulligan in the late 1980s. "I wish I would be able to play with Gerry now," he told me. "I would have gotten it so much better. I feel really lucky that he recognized I could do that with him, because when I hear anything from that time, I feel I was quite green. I had a lot of nice times just going up to his house and hanging out."

DeRosa met Mulligan in the late '70s while still a student at Jersey City State College (now New Jersey City University). "I would go up to his house in Connecticut and help him, copying parts, assembling the books, proofreading," he recalled to me in an interview for my book *Jazz Notes: Interviews Across the Generations.* "It was a fortunate experience for me. When he put together a rehearsal, I played drums."

Mulligan's "real wish," Luther said, "was a Broadway show. He would say, 'We're not up here just to fulfill our whatever. We're here to entertain.' He saw it that way, and that plays a very important role in everything he did."

"He loved the songwriters," Charlap said. "He loved the architecture of the songs. Yet, he's a jazz composer. You hear those influences. You also hear Ellington, of course, and Lester Young in a big way. Gerry was such a linear improviser. He had a different way of hearing. And he was a fantastic improviser. He had a very distinct melodic language that makes him so special. It's not just understanding the language that's around him or even regurgitating it in an original way. He wrote the book on jazz counterpoint."

Mulligan's affinity for Broadway created a somewhat instant rapport with another of his pianists, Harold Danko. Just before joining Mulligan in 1980, Danko wrote an unsuccessful off-Broadway musical. "It was called *A Matter of Opinion,*" he recalled to me. "It lasted about eleven performances downtown at the Players Theatre. It bombed. But Gerry and I talked about that, and one day, later on, when he was doing tunes like 'I Never Was a Young Man,' he would say, 'I think I always wanted to be on 42nd Street, but I ended up on 52nd Street.'"

Ted Rosenthal, a pianist who played with Mulligan from 1992 until Mulligan's death in 1996, also believes Mulligan would have liked to have written a Broadway show. "Melody was clearly paramount to him," Rosenthal told me. The Broadway side of Mulligan, Rosenthal added, "really came through in some of his later songs. They were unabashedly very melodic and very romantic, almost much more like Broadway show tunes than jazz tunes. We did a couple of things with Wynton Marsalis, and I would hear Wynton comment, 'Oh, those melodies,' kind of like he couldn't shake them out of his head. Gerry's melodies were songs that had some kind of substance. Whatever that intangible quality is, he definitely had that. So that melodic characteristic in his writing and his playing was indispensable to his style."

Pianist Mitch Forman knew DeRosa in high school on Long Island, where DeRosa's father was a pioneering jazz educator who started the first public-school jazz band. "Richie introduced me to Gerry," Forman recalled. "I was just a kid, but Gerry was very supportive, nurturing. It was probably my first major jazz gig. It was an amazing opportunity." The highlight of Forman's three years with Mulligan was a trip to Italy. "He took Richie and me. We stayed with Franca's friends, Lulu and Luigi, and he produced a record for me that I recently put out. It was half my music on piano and half his music."

The record, *Lost and Found*, was released on the Marsis Jazz label in 2010. C. Michael Bailey reviewed one of the tracks—Mulligan's composition "Butterflies with Hiccups"—for the website All About Jazz. The composition, he wrote, "possesses elements of 1920s jazz piano, stride, ragtime, and mainstream. Forman's playing captures the title perfectly with his offtime, almost loping playing, centering around an ostensible waltz meter. Forman leaves very little space for silence, but he does not do so in too wordy a way as Art Tatum often did. His playing does have a dense economy where no notes are wasted. This recording is a gem from beginning to end, teetering on the crown of 'Butterflies with Hiccups.'"

When Danko joined Mulligan, he was acutely aware that "Gerry got famous for the pianoless groups, and he really didn't need me. So I tried to stay out of his way. The nice thing, though: As trust developed, I played quite a lot. At first, it was a matter of learning what Gerry really wanted. I think once I got that, then it could go anywhere. Gerry was an arranger before anything, but once that gets into place, then you can become creative. It was a kind of discipline I learned and got to enjoy."

In *Jazz Notes: Interviews Across the Generations*, another pianist, Bill Mays, who performed and recorded with Mulligan in the '80s, recalled playing one song in which "I knew I'd only get one chorus, and, on another song, I'd only get eight bars. At first, I felt kind of limited until I really got into his mind and the way he thought about music and presenting music. It taught me a really valuable lesson about making smaller, more concise statements musically." In 2014, Mays added, "I learned how to say more in a small period of time. Then, on some pieces, he would encourage me to stretch it and go for several choruses. His artistic choices were always with great taste and balance."

In a quartet with piano, said Charlap, "He didn't want you to be Bud Powell. And he didn't want you to be Oscar Peterson either. He wanted you to be another voice as an arranger. He wanted instant arrangements. He liked it when you weren't thinking about piano but about the whole being bigger than its parts. And thinking about contributing like an arranger would, not thinking about the conventions of what jazz piano was supposed to be. I had to figure that out, because I was a young guy in my early twenties, and all I wanted to do was figure out how Bud Powell or Bill Evans or Oscar Peterson played."

In a review of a 1989 album, *Lonesome Boulevard* (A&M), AllMusic reviewer Michael G. Nastos singled out Charlap's piano playing. "A young Bill Charlap on the piano," wrote Nastos, "proved to be a perfect foil for the baritone saxophonist's leaner notions. Charlap is also quite substantive, never grabbing the spotlight for himself, but tastefully adding chord progressions and comping to Mulligan's world-class musings." The album, according to Nastos, is "a beautiful statement of where the refined, seasoned veteran of cool jazz was at in the later years of his life."

Rosenthal joined Mulligan during a European tour of Mulligan's "Re-Birth of the Cool" band, a '90s update of the original. "My role there," Rosenthal said, "was somewhat limited by the arrangements that didn't call for too much piano. We had all those instruments, and the original pianist was John Lewis, who played in a very spare way. All those factors, combined with my historical knowledge of him playing with a pianoless group, made me wonder, 'Well, how much does he really want to hear from me?' He told me when I was playing too much. In that group, my role was supportive."

As a teenager, Rosenthal had taken some piano lessons from Danko, who recalled taking his former student up to Connecticut to audition for Mulligan: "I said to Ted, 'Remember, Gerry's a piano player. He knows about harmony. Stay out of his way. He doesn't need you.'"

Once Rosenthal started doing a steadier diet of gigs with Mulligan's quartet, however, "We began to have a musical relationship, interacting—trading, passing a melody back and forth. He was always listening," Rosenthal said. "He was always playing from both a performer's and arranger/composer's perspective. So he was always listening for ideas that would then spark his ideas or feed ideas that he expected us to respond to or get out of the way of or whatever might be called for."

With drummers, said Ron Vincent, who played with Mulligan mostly in the '90s, "he couldn't really explain what he wanted. But he knew what it was when he heard it. He sure as hell knew what he didn't want. He had the biggest musical ears. I've never been around someone who could hear things like that. He could hear it and immediately know what it was and say, 'No, no, I don't want that. I want this.'"

"He was able to think like an arranger," said Charlap, in earlier interviews for *Jazz Notes: Interviews Across the Generations*. "He was one of the most important arrangers in the history of music. He had an ear that could hear Stravinsky as well as James P. Johnson."

Bassist Dean Johnson described Mulligan as "one of the famous cantankerous guys, and he had a right to be. He liked good pianos. One time I remember in Brazil, we showed up and there was a Yamaha electric grand. Gerry went nuts. 'But it's a grand,' they said. It's impossible to find pianos in Rio, but they were able to find a piano and bring it in." (I remember being at StoryTowne, a New York City club on 58th & Madison, in the late '70s, to hear Mulligan's quartet. He was clearly upset with the tuning of the piano and commented on it between every tune. Finally, in exasperation, he said, 'Now, I know why I played with a pianoless quartet,' and the piano player, Derek Smith, nearly fell off his stool.)

Danko remembered Mulligan being agitated with Luther for using a bow during a high-profile television show appearance in Italy with the popular vocalist Ornella Vanoni. "It was Gerry, Frank on bass, Butch Miles on drums, and me," Danko said. "The TV show came off fine, although we had to play shorter solos. The next day we got on the bus, and Gerry was really grumpy that day. He said, 'I'm pissed off. Does anyone know why I'm pissed off?' And then there was silence. We thought we'd played pretty well. 'That's one of the reasons I'm pissed off,' he continued, 'because nobody knows why I'm pissed off.' Then, he got next to Frank and screamed at Frank, 'You know I don't like it when you bow solos!' He kind of implied to Frank that 'You're lucky it was a *good* solo.'"

Saxophonist Ted Nash remembered Mulligan as "a bit of a control freak. On the bus rides, he didn't want you to listen to music on earphones too loud. He hated that. One time, we were playing a festival, and [trumpeter] Freddie Hubbard was playing. We gave Freddie a ride on the bus, and Freddie, at some point, put his headphones on and started listening to music, and Gerry told him to turn it off. We were all dying." Forman said Mulligan "hated hearing music in a restaurant. I remember sometimes he would ask them to turn it down or shut it off."

Drummer Vincent conceded that Mulligan was "a hard guy to deal with at times. But he was also very fair. Once, we were on the road for two weeks, and in the middle of the tour, my back was killing me. When we got to the hotel, there was a knock on the door, and there's this guy standing there. 'Mr. Mulligan sent me up,' he said. 'I'm a masseuse.' He would do things like that out of the blue. And he always took us to great restaurants.

"When he was difficult, there was usually a good reason for it. I remember one time when we had a concert in Long Island City a place called Angelo's, a catering hall. We were going to play a half dozen tunes during a meal for the prime minister of Italy. I get there, and I'm going through the front door, and the caterer says, 'No, no, no, you can't come in the front door; you have to go through the back door.' I was used to this from doing weddings in the early '80s. I didn't budge; I just stood there and waited. A limo pulls up, and Gerry gets out. 'What are you doing here?' he asked. 'You should be set up.' He walked up to the caterer and said, 'We're coming through the front door.' The caterer said, 'No, musicians come in through the back.' Gerry said, 'I'll tell you what. We're going to leave now. We're going to go home, and, when the prime minister shows up, you explain to him why we're not here.' The caterer said, 'Come on in.'"

Luther recalled playing at Hopper's once when vocalist Anita O'Day was in the audience. "She'd been known to put away a few," Luther said. "She was feeling good, and Gerry said, 'Anita O'Day's in the audience. I'd like to invite her up to sing a number with me.' So, she gets up there and says she'd like to sing 'You Are the Sunshine of My Life,' which was a big hit at the time for Stevie Wonder. And Gerry goes, 'Oh, no, no, I don't want to do that. Let's play 'Pennies from Heaven.'

"At this point in time, the place really quiets down. Tom Fay's playing piano, and we're just sitting there. She starts singing 'You Are the Sunshine of My Life,' so we just start backing her up, and Gerry comes in with 'Pennies from Heaven.' So then we start backing up Gerry. It was so unbelievable. I don't remember what happened. I don't remember how it ended. All I remember is looking at the audience, and the waiters were frozen. No one moved."

A memorable Hopper's gig for guitarist John Scofield occurred when "[guitarist] Jim Hall, my idol, and Paul Desmond came in. It was a packed house. Somebody had saved a table for them, but it was right in front of the bandstand, which was really weird for all of us. I was so nervous, I couldn't even play. Gerry got pissed off and was yelling at the rhythm section—'You're rushing!' and stuff like that. I think it was because they had sat Paul and Jim right in front of us. And Paul and Jim seemed a little bit uncomfortable because they realized what was going on."

Bassist Dean Johnson said Mulligan "could talk on any subject; he was a voracious reader." Forman would watch him zip through *The New York Times* crossword puzzle. "He would just barrel through them, in ink pen. He'd go across, down, across, and do the whole thing." Mulligan loved history. His favorite book was *The Martyrdom of Man* by Winwood Reade, an unconventional history of the world written in 1872. Mulligan said he considered it "a breakthrough book, a fascinating book that offered another point of view altogether on the evolution of Western civilization and how the Western and African and Oriental civilizations overlapped—something our history books didn't cover at all."

12

'I FORGOT HE WAS FAMOUS FOR A REASON'

In 1978, Mulligan decided to revive a version of the Concert Jazz Band. "I wanted to have my own band again," he said. "Franca was really the prime mover, because she realized that's what I wanted to do, but I was hesitant to take this on again. She realized how hard it was for me to sell myself to agents and promoters and, as a consequence, I was usually taken advantage of. When Franca started dealing with these people, my whole relationship with agents changed. They didn't have me, the easy pushover."

Franca knew where to draw the line, though, between business and music. "I didn't want to make any decisions that dealt with the music," she emphasized to me. "I had nothing to do with the hiring and firing, the quality of the musicians. Those were all Gerry's decisions. He knew the pace on the road: 'Yes, we can do that. No, we can't do that.' So it was like a family. But I was always talking to the businesspeople. I would say, 'This is the way we have to do it. Take it or leave it.' Musicians will play no matter what, because they feel the responsibility of the audience. They always need to find a solution, but they have to put their foot down, and I was the one putting the foot down for him."

When Mulligan was in the process of assembling musicians for his new big band, he received a unique opportunity for a rehearsal venue. "We were on the porch of our Rowayton cottage with the chief of the Club Mediterranean village in Guadeloupe," Franca recalled. "A musician himself, he was in touch with jazz musicians because he was inviting people to go to Club Med and play there. "Gerry said he was putting together this big band, but he wanted to put them in a place for one week where they could wash [out] the other music they [had] in their heads and just rehearse and be ready for a tour in Europe. But he told the chief—his name was Bernard— 'I cannot afford a studio in New York to keep them like that for a week.' Bernard said, 'Don't worry about it. You come to Guadeloupe. I pay for everything. You come down there. You rehearse your band for one week. You don't even have to perform. At the end of the week, if you'd like to make a performance, it is up to you. But just for me to advertise that Gerry Mulligan is coming down to put together his new big band and is rehearsing down there—it's enough.' He paid for the transportation and for everything, and also gave beads to the musicians so they could have some drinks. So we went. It was a holiday for the musicians. The people were outside this big room, listening to the band rehearsing. The last night, the band performed. It was great. The musicians were absolutely together."

The new big band was an expanded version of the original '60s Concert Jazz Band. "I added a fourth trumpet and a fifth saxophone," Mulligan said. "The sound of the band with those couple of extra horns was that much stronger for playing in big places. The band had more impact. There's a geometric equation with trumpets. Three trumpets is a certain loudness; a fourth trumpet adds a great deal to the power of the three. It gave us the possibility of a much more loud ensemble. This concert jazz band was a much more subtle instrumentation, geared really to the concert hall, not geared to the festival atmosphere at all. And I added piano, which makes it a lot easier for the rhythm section. So, all together, it was quite a different-sounding band."

In a July 1976 interview in *Down Beat*, Mulligan had been asked by writer Arnold Jay Smith if he ever felt the piano was "missing" from his earlier groups. "When the band was in front of an audience," he said, "I never noticed it. But as I listen to those old recordings, I realize what a strain it must have been when we were in the studio. How those bass and drum players had to work! The atmosphere is quite sterile in studios, as opposed to clubs. On second hearing, I wished for a guitar or piano. Which one [of those] depends on the thinking of the player of the instrument in question."

Made up mostly of young musicians, the band toured Europe and made an appearance in early 1979 at StoryTowne, the club George Wein opened on East 58th Street in New York. In February 1979, *Down Beat* described the performance as "refreshing and alive with some of the finest side people Mulligan could muster." Mulligan told the magazine that the band had had only two weeks of rehearsal, "but we've worked the road for another three. We'll be doing a tour of the West and Southwest in the near future." In June 1979, the band made a surprise appearance at the Newport Jazz Festival in New York before an audience at Carnegie Hall that was expecting to see Mulligan's quartet.

Rich DeRosa was working as Mulligan's assistant when the band was formed, and he became the drummer. "His writing was very adventurous," DeRosa told me. "It was bebop, it was swing, it was classical, it was improvised—everything. When we played with Gerry, he would call it a show. We weren't just playing notes; we were playing like a chef preparing a meal. The pacing was very important. With Gerry, every tune he selected was a new place to go. It was a big stylistic journey. And no matter where it went, there was always a melodic thread." Saxophonist Ted Nash, who joined the band in 1980, emphasized to me that Mulligan "knew how to set up the song. He told anecdotes and stories to the audience—like the story about his composition 'K-4 Pacific.' He would just tell this whole story about the train coming into the station. It was the first time I had worked with somebody who could make the audience feel part of the music."

DeRosa felt Mulligan was very theatrical. "He was entranced with the theater. He loved the theater. He loved to write songs. That was his inherent melodicism. He played the saxophone like a singer would sing the lyric."

Trombonist Alan Raph was a link to the original Concert Jazz Band. He played with the new band at StoryTowne and in Guadeloupe for a week of rehearsals. "The saxes," he recalled, "were really, really good players and so were the trumpets, especially the lead trumpet player, Laurie Frink. And Mitch Forman was wonderful on piano." However, the one thing that was missing, in Raph's mind, was the presence of Bob Brookmeyer. "We missed Brookmeyer. That was the difference, from my point of view." Raph joined the band in the fall of 1978, but he had a standing six-week gig every summer with Frankie Avalon. Although his spot wasn't open for a return, he did appear on the band's one recording, *Walk on the Water* (DRG: 1980), which won a Grammy Award for Best Jazz Instrumental Performance.

John McNeil was a thirty-year-old trumpeter whom Mulligan tried to hire for the band, "but I was playing with Horace Silver, and I wasn't available," McNeil said. "However, I wound up being a sub. I was in awe. I tried to listen and learn as much as I could and ask him as many questions I could get away with. I owe a lot of what I am as a writer to him."

McNeil believes that Mulligan, in many ways, "is overlooked in what his contributions were and how good he was as a writer. Some people view his music as more of an older school, and they really don't appreciate the genius of it."

An example of Mulligan's genius arose when the band was preparing for a July 1982 Kool Jazz Festival concert with Mel Tormé and Sarah Vaughan. "We were serving as the big band behind Tormé," McNeil recalled. "Tormé learned to write arrangements, but he really didn't know how to do it. Everything was really overwritten. When we started playing these things in rehearsal, Gerry said, 'Let's go back and change this, change this rhythm, change the trumpets, and so on. He worked his way through the chart after one hearing. I watched him—he wasn't making notes. He rewrote it all the way through. And then it just really came to life. When Mel Tormé heard the result, he just said, 'Man, thanks for the arranging lesson.' Mulligan just smiled at him. He went through six or seven charts and rewrote them all, at sight, in real time. He only had to rewrite it once. Afterwards, someone said, 'I forgot he was famous for a reason.' He was a genius. It was the most virtuoso display I've ever seen. I've never seen that before or since."

Raph also remembered the concert with Tormé and Vaughan. "We played our stuff, and then Mel Tormé came out, and the band accompanied him. I had to move over to tuba for Tormé. And then the second half was Sarah—an older Sarah, but with that great voice."

On June 29, 1982, the band performed at Carnegie Hall with Tormé and George Shearing in a concert that was later broadcast on National Public Radio's *Jazz Alive!* series. No recording of the concert was available, however, until twenty-three years later, when Concord Records released *The Classic Concert Live*. *Jazz Times*'s Christopher Loudon described it as "one of those rare nights when seasoned masters, each at the top of his game, converge to create an inimitably tight unit while remaining individually determined to rise to the competitive brilliance of their friendly stage rivals." The original concert was two hours in length, reduced to sixty-five minutes on the recording, but Loudon said it "still captures the magic and majesty of the evening."

Pianist Harold Danko, who followed Forman as Mulligan's keyboardist, believes Mulligan was "an arranger before anything. But once that got into place, you could become creative. It was a kind of discipline I learned and got to really enjoy."

DeRosa believes that music "needs to have complexity and simplicity. Young people are more enamored with complexity. They become engrossed in technical things and forget people have to listen to it. Gerry cut through all that. 'This doesn't feel good,' he would say. He loved to tinker. We'd be rehearsing, and we'd think we got what he wanted, and he'd get rid of something or come in with another version. It was like Einstein fiddling around."

In *Jazz Notes: Interviews Across the Generations*, trombonist Keith O'Quinn told me that Mulligan "would rewrite things constantly. Sometimes, we would have rehearsals where we would do nothing but rehearse backgrounds to use behind the soloists."

Mulligan's compositions, said Gary Smulyan, "have beautiful melodies. He was really, deep down, a melodicist. His melodies are just exquisite. That's become a lost art in terms of young guys playing that way today. You don't hear a lot of young musicians playing in that style. They're playing very vertically in terms of harmony. They're not really playing beautiful melodies across the chords. The direction's changed a little bit. I really miss that aspect of improvisation, especially in young musicians. Gerry was the supreme melodicist. There really wasn't anybody better. His sound was perfect for how he played—the perfect blend of everything."

When college bands play Mulligan's music today, something gets lost, in Danko's opinion. "The thing they don't get about his music that's really important," he said, "is that his big band was a very soft big band. He wanted the fullness, but he wanted the big band to be able to play softly. Hearing a student band trying to do his music the first time, it just doesn't sound like his music. One of the difficulties is that he wrote for the guys in the band, and he picked people carefully for the blend and how full and deep it could sound at soft volumes. The younger bands today will nail all the notes, but it will be too loud. The music is kind of like chamber music. It's more difficult than it sounds."

Nash first saw the big band perform in 1979 at the Saratoga Jazz Festival. "I was there with [bassist] Chuck Israels's big band. We were going to perform later in the day after Gerry's band. His band was just swinging so hard. Everything he played was just so perfectly chosen. He never wasted a note. I felt almost a little intimidated by it. I remember seeing all of these cats I'd never seen before up there playing and swinging. I was nineteen, and I feel it's taken me a couple of generations of my own life to sort of understand what it is to edit yourself so well while you're playing and not play a bunch of extra notes. Everything he played had meaning, and everything had a purpose. He was really one of the greatest improvising composers. His music was as if he were composing all the time, rather than just playing solos. I think that's what we're missing a lot with today's jazz musicians. His big-band arranging was as close to perfect as you could get."

About a year after the Saratoga performance, Mulligan was looking for a lead alto player for the band, and Nash auditioned. Mulligan, Nash remembered, "was a little eccentric; he could lose his temper; and he could be particular about the way we rehearsed. But he was very likable. I thought he was a very accessible guy. He was intelligent and funny. He wouldn't have this kind of pretense—'I'm the leader, and you're the sideman.' As a musician, I felt I wasn't fully developed enough to bring what I thought I should bring to that music. I was still trying to find myself, my own identity. It was a great experience for me to play with the band because I was able to settle down. He created this environment so that we could play all this great music. The way he played was very simple in some ways, but it was so intuitive."

Walk on the Water was the only recording of the rejuvenated big band. Reviewing the album for AllMusic, Scott Yanow pointed out that Mulligan "has had few opportunities to record with a big band since his Concert Jazz Band broke up in 1963, a real pity considering how talented a composer and arranger he has been." The album contained four Mulligan originals: "For an Unfinished Woman," "Song for Strayhorn," "42nd & Broadway," and the title track. On both "Walk on the Water" and "42nd & Broadway," Mulligan played soprano sax. Other tracks on the album included "Angelica," an original composition by Mitchel Forman, and the standards "Across the Track Blues" (Duke Ellington) and "I'm Getting Sentimental Over You" (George Bassman/Ned Washington).

Raymond Horricks, writing about the band in his book *Gerry Mulligan's Ark*, described it as having "a more robust attack than any previous Mulligan group. There is more excitement generated within its ensemble, and young and contrasting ideas are allowed to roam freely through the solo choruses. The important identification marks of his writing remain, with saxophones still dominating the theme statements and still frequently a baritone lead. But there are some sharper angles to the contours of his lines now, and the brasses, in punctuating these angles, are allowed to blow with a forthright brilliance not normally associated with the more mellow, integrated Mulligan sounds of previous years. However, this clarity and precision are the same; and if the decibels have increased, then there is also a lot of room for delicacy and a kind of magisterial gracefulness inside the overall balance . . . There is always the swing—pragmatic, provoking and unadorned, undeterred no matter what the time signature."

When the band had its "official" opening at StoryTowne, *Down Beat*, in February 1979, described "the look" on Mulligan's face as being "one of sublime relaxation . . . The tunes are familiar from the 1960-1964 edition of Mulligan's big band, but some of the charts differ. Some are expanded charts of the sextet he fronted recently, while others are from the old book even down to the fills." Singled out were trumpeter Barry Ries, trombonists Keith O'Quinn and Dave Glenn, and tenor saxophonist Gary Keller. Forman had not joined the band yet, so the pianist was his predecessor, Tom Fay.

Lee Jeske, reviewing the album for *Down Beat* in April 1981, said that having Mulligan "at the helm of a big band is a welcome delight. Mulligan's lilting baritone and soprano tones and terse, lyrical improvisations are even more effective when floating on a cushion of flutes and flugelhorns. The ensemble voicings here (notably on the original title tune) weave a lush broadloom of sound." Jeske felt the "spectacular arrangement of 'I'm Getting Sentimental Over You' is the album's highlight." He also singled out the solos of pianist Forman and trumpeter Tom Harrell.

Harrell told me the Newport Jazz Festival appearance at Carnegie Hall was "really special" to him. "The concept of melodic improvising was brought home to me. It was a great evening. I've been listening to Gerry's music since the '50s. I was always drawn to his concept, to the relaxation of his swing. He contributed an adventuresome spirit and an awareness of the tradition of having the courage to explore musical horizons. He could go from a chamber kind of sound to a shouting big-band sound. He was very spontaneous and could contribute new ideas very effectively."

The Grammy Award for *Walk on the Water* was Mulligan's first, although *Birth of the Cool* is in the Grammy Hall of Fame. The albums *The Age of Steam* and *Soft Lights & Sweet Music* with Scott Hamilton had been nominated, and Mulligan's composition "For an Unfinished Woman," from *Walk on the Water*, was nominated for Best Instrumental Performance by a Group.

Mulligan was disappointed that *Little Big Horn*, an album recorded on the GRP label in 1981 and made shortly after *Walk on the Water*, did not receive recognition from the Grammy judges. "It was kind of ignored," he said, "because people put you in pigeonholes, and you're not allowed out. *Little Big Horn* had a current kind of rhythm section with stuff like synthesizers. But to me, it was basically a straight-ahead album with different rhythm treatments. But it was kind of perceived as a rock-oriented album. As a consequence, it got lost in the cracks."

The album consisted of six new Mulligan compositions, including a Mulligan vocal on "I Never Was a Young Man," which AllMusic's Yanow called "rare but very effective." The musicians included two pianists, Dave Grusin and Richard Tee; two bassists, Jay Leonhart (acoustic) and Anthony Jackson (electric); Buddy Williams on drums; Marvin Stamm and Alan Rubin on trumpet; Keith O'Quinn on trombone; Lou Marini on alto saxophone; and Michael Brecker on tenor saxophone.

"We had dynamite guys in the ensemble," Mulligan said. "We started out taking the quartet into the studio and recording a lot of the repertoire that hadn't been recorded, and it never really came to life. Dave [Grusin] and I talked it over and decided it wasn't going to work. So we revamped our thinking about it. We came up with the idea of doing a setting for each piece, which the album is. There's not one band on it. Going from piece to piece, it's different instrumentation, different players, and a different atmosphere. And it fits.

"There are a couple of things in there that are real favorites of mine. There was one piece we wound up calling 'Bright Angel Falls' because Franca and I had done something with the quartet in Phoenix, and we drove up to see the Grand Canyon. And I saw a place called Bright Angel Falls, and I loved that. [The music] was kind of a blues with a hint of gospel orientation. Just as we started to play the piece in the studio, Dave looked out of the window of the control room, and he saw Booker T. He said, 'Come on in, come on in. I've got something here for you to play.' And he sits Booker T. down at the piano, and Dave goes over to the Fender Rhodes, and Booker T. just tore the thing up. It really came out great."

In 1982, Mulligan was interviewed by Billy Taylor on *CBS Sunday Morning*. Taylor asked him about what it was like to be on the road again with a band. "A band," Mulligan said, "is a family. You have to be able to function together closely, preferably over a long period of time, so your personality traits, the ability to get along, to be able to give, to dominate and be part of the group are very important . . . My wife and I handle this like a small family business. The main thing is, it should be fun to do."

Eleven years later, Taylor and Mulligan made an album together, *Live at MCG* (MCG Jazz), and it was clear they were having fun. It was recorded at the Manchester's Craftsmen's Guild in Pittsburgh and featured Mulligan with Taylor, Chip Jackson on bass, and Carl Allen on drums. "Baritone saxophonist Mulligan," wrote *Jazz Times*'s Mike Joyce in October 2007, "sounds perfectly at ease with the company he's keeping and with a mostly standards repertoire. Beginning with 'Stompin' at the Savoy,' the arrangements inspire plenty of unfussy swing and spirited exchanges . . . 'Line for Lyons' is distinguished by the trio's rambunctious brand of interplay and Taylor's jaunty chromaticism and cascading runs . . ." All About Jazz's Woodrow Wilkins, on December 7, 2007, said the album served a "dual purpose: It entertains while providing a subliminal lesson in improvisation, a hallmark of jazz past and present. Having these two masters work together enhances the experience."

13

'SCHUBERT! BEETHOVEN! MULLIGAN!'

Mulligan was initially reluctant to delve too seriously into the world of classical composing. After David Amram began working with the New York Philharmonic in 1966 and '67, he recalled Mulligan telling him, "I guess we can't hang out anymore and jam."

Trying to convince Mulligan that the saxophonist would be well accepted by "serious" composers, Amram took Mulligan to a performance by the Juilliard Wind Orchestra in the spring of 1967. "They were performing my horn concerto," Amram recalled to me, "with John Cerminaro as a soloist on French horn and John Chambers conducting. I remember sitting there with Gerry and telling him, 'Even though I am now the first composer-in-residence with the New York Philharmonic, I feel weird being here at Juilliard. My degree is in European history from George Washington University. I never even finished the Manhattan School of Music.' And Gerry said, 'Don't feel weird. I never even finished high school.'

"There were all these kids who had musically arrived; they had just gotten into Juilliard. Gerry looked around and said, 'I wish I could do something like this.' I said, 'Gerry, you're already doing something like that. Everything you write is like that. Just take your music that you're writing and expand on it.

"After the concert, we went backstage, and I introduced Gerry to some of the kids in the orchestra, and they freaked out—'Gerry Mulligan!' They were so excited. It's as if I had brought Arturo Toscanini. They understood and appreciated him. I think he was expecting to get this snob-ola treatment. The students were all thrilled to meet Gerry because they respected his unique musicality as much as I did. And anyone with ears could hear, whenever he played with or wrote for bands, that he was already a serious composer. When he asked me what influenced me to write symphonic music, I told him that the music and the spirit of Gesualdo, Bach, Mozart, Brahms, Berlioz, Dvorak, Stravinsky, Bartók, Gershwin, Ellington, Monk, and Gerry's own nonet were all I needed to inspire me to find my own voice."

Among Mulligan classical projects in the '70s were a performance with the New Haven Symphony Orchestra in 1975 in New Haven, Connecticut, and a commission by the Canadian Broadcasting Company for Canadian composer Harry Freedman to write a symphonic work in honor of Mulligan's fiftieth birthday. The saxophone concerto "Celebration" was performed by the CBS Symphony Orchestra with Mulligan as guest soloist. It was also subsequently performed with other symphony orchestras. Gail Dixon, in her book *The Music of Harry Freedman*, described the Freedman concerto as "a jazz-oriented work for saxophone and full symphony orchestra. While embracing some of the principles of mainstream serious music, 'Celebration' gives full expression to Freedman's predilection for jazz."

The real turning point, though, in Mulligan's involvement with classical music was a chance meeting with Zubin Mehta, then conductor of the New York Philharmonic, on a cross-country flight from Los Angeles to New York in 1982. Franca Mulligan recalled being in the L.A. airport when "a good-looking woman comes up and says, 'Gerry, maybe you don't remember me, but I know you. I am Nancy Mehta, Zubin Mehta's wife. When I was in college, I was playing your music on the college radio station. I would like to introduce Zubin to you.'

"Once we were on the flight" Franca continued, "I said, 'Gerry, go introduce yourself to Zubin Mehta.' So, he went, and he came back five hours later. Gerry said Zubin asked him why he didn't write for a symphony orchestra. 'Don't you have a big band?' he asked. 'How many people are in the big band?' When Gerry said from thirteen to eighteen, Zubin replied, 'Multiply by five and you have a symphony orchestra.'

"That took the block away from Gerry. In the meantime, Zubin asked him if he would come and play "Bolero" with the Philharmonic. Gerry asked him to send him the part, and the next day Zubin called. We weren't home, and Zubin whistled the whole part on the answering machine. So Gerry didn't see the part until he went to rehearsal."

Mulligan played "Bolero" with the Philharmonic in May 1982 in Lincoln Center's Avery Fisher Hall. There was a mishap during what was supposed to be Mulligan's first appearance with the Philharmonic. "He came with the small soprano sax," Mehta recalled to me. "And, as he was going to start to play, one of the metal keys snapped. He couldn't play. He was so embarrassed, and the orchestra was embarrassed, too, because they were tickled that he came to play. The next performance, he came and played, and it was fine."

Covering one of the concerts for *The New York Times,* classical music critic Donal Henahan wrote on May 7, 1982, that "Mr. Mehta's choice for a finale to the season was Ravel's 'Bolero.' One footnote in the Philharmonic's history must be recorded—sitting in the saxophone section was Gerry Mulligan, the eminent jazzman. It seems that Mr. Mehta met Mr. Mulligan on an airplane and invited him to sit in for the occasion."

The Christian Science Monitor's Thor Eckert Jr. reported that "There was something startling, electrifying about the saxophone solo in the weekend performances of Ravel's 'Bolero' that Zubin Mehta directed to close the New York Philharmonic season. The tune rang out with blazing authority; it was played with a freedom, a nuance, an insinuating thrust that one hardly expects from a classical player and that one almost never encounters in any orchestra . . . At the end, when the soloists stood for their bows, the reason that sax solo had been so noteworthy was revealed. No one quite looks like the white bearded and maned Gerry Mulligan, one of jazz's greats. And no one sounds like him either . . . Clearly, Ravel "heard" jazz when he wrote this piece. It takes a jazz artist to remind us of something that bad or lazy tradition has made us forget or ignore. Mulligan's phrasing offered the effortless insight that comes from a lifetime of living with a certain type or style of music."

Mehta told me he considers Mulligan "one of the great jazz exponents of his time. He would come to rehearsals in New York and follow the score, and he would ask questions. I loved our friendship, but it was too short because he passed on."

Shortly after the "Bolero" performance, Mulligan began work on an extended symphonic piece that would become his "Entente for Saxophone and Orchestra." According to Franca, he decided to take a sabbatical off the road and concentrate on writing "Entente" in Milan. "One day," she recalled, "he said, 'I'm going to La Scala because I cannot hear the orchestra in my head anymore. I have to go back there and put the orchestra back in my head.' La Scala was ten minutes' walking distance from where we lived in Milan."

Riccardo Muti was rehearsing *Turandot* with the orchestra when Mulligan and Franca entered the hall. He recalled his reaction in the *Listen: Gerry Mulligan* video. "Suddenly, I was attracted by a presence that I felt in the hall," he said. "I turned, and I saw this beautiful person, almost like a prophet—certainly a face that impresses you. I didn't stop conducting, but I turned and I thought, 'I know this face.' And then, at the end of the rehearsal, he came to me with his wife, and I realized, before he introduced himself, that it was Gerry Mulligan. And I must confess that I had a deep emotion that this person—one of the idols of my youth—was there in La Scala. I saw him several times in La Scala during rehearsals, and so I learned how important it was for him to come to La Scala to listen to the orchestra because, being also a very important composer, he came to rehearsals to study several combinations of sounds. He studied the music of the composers of the past and of the classical music of today. He was very open to the world of composition because composition was one of the reasons of his music existence. I read it in his eyes."

Mulligan completed "Entente for Saxophone and Orchestra" in 1984 and first performed it in June of that year in Treviso, Italy, with the Filarmonia Veneta, conducted by Rico Saccani. In October 1984, he performed both "Entente" and "The Sax Chronicles" with the London Symphony Orchestra conducted by Michel Sasson. "Entente" was performed twice in the U.S. in August 1985—at the Hollywood Bowl by the Los Angeles Philharmonic, conducted by Erich Kunzel, and in New York by the American Composers Orchestra, conducted by Dennis Russell Davies. His first performance of "Entente" with Mehta occurred in 1987 in Tel Aviv with the Israel Philharmonic. His quartet also performed "K-4 Pacific" with the Israel Philharmonic. In the program notes, written by Phillip Ramey, Mulligan was described as "not only among the most respected figures in modern jazz, but also one of the most versatile."

When Mulligan came out for an encore, he was surprised by the appearance of violinist Itzhak Perlman, who had performed earlier in the program. Perlman joined his quartet to play an improvised version of Hoagy Carmichael's "Georgia on My Mind." The other members of the quartet for that performance were Harold Danko, piano; Dean Johnson, bass; and Butch Miles, drums.

In 1987, Mulligan recorded an album called *Symphonic Dreams* with Erich Kunzel and the Houston Symphony Orchestra on the Pro Arts label. *Down Beat*'s John McDonough, in July 1988, wrote that Mulligan "had made the sort of album every jazz musician seems to want to do at least once. He's tried to mix the linguistics of jazz with the grammar of the symphony. Although he hasn't managed to reconcile their polarities, he's still produced an attractive collection of Third Stream exercises that, among other things, cast some original Mulligan tunes in the manner of Bach, Mozart, Debussy, Brahms, and Stravinsky." Third Stream, as noted earlier, is a term created by Gunther Schuller to describe a combination of classical music and jazz.

In the 1989 *Down Beat* interview with Michael Bourne, Mulligan talked about *Symphonic Dreams*, which contained "K-4 Pacific" and another Mulligan composition, "Song for Strayhorn," along with his "Sax Chronicles" and "Entente." "I work two ways with a symphony now," Mulligan explained to Bourne. "I'll do concerts as a soloist where I'll play part of the 'Chronicles' and that's it. But a good many concerts, like the one with Zubin Mehta and the Israel Philharmonic last year, I'll work as a soloist, plus have other music the quartet plays with me." In "The Sax Chronicles," Harry Freedman arranged Mulligan's melodies in the styles of classical composers such as Bach, Brahms, and Mozart.

In December 1989, Mulligan and his quartet performed "Entente for Saxophone and Orchestra" and "K-4 Pacific" in four performances with the New York Philharmonic, conducted by Zubin Mehta, in Lincoln Center's Avery Fisher Hall. Previewing these performances in the November 19, 1989, issue of *The New York Times,* Mark Tucker characterized them as an attempt to "seek a reconciliation of symphonic and jazz forces, attempting to turn a potentially hazardous partnership into a harmonious coalition.

"In mixing classical and jazz practice," Tucker continued, "one of the most problematic areas is rhythm. Many conservatory-trained players have difficulty achieving the relaxed yet precisely timed phrasing characteristic of jazz. They might effortlessly toss off the most complex rhythmic combinations imaginable, but ask them to swing straight eighth notes and many will draw a blank . . . In 'Entente,' Mr. Mulligan attempted to steer around this problem: 'I wrote rhythms that symphonic players are used to. The orchestra has its own language for swing. In every era composers used various devices to achieve that rhythmic momentum—that's what I tapped into.' As it turns out, much of 'Entente' is based on gentle, undulating bass patterns more characteristic of Latin jazz —even Ravel's 'Bolero'—than straight-ahead swing. The orchestra's rhythms remain minimally syncopated, only occasionally breaking out into figures reminiscent of the big bands Mr. Mulligan arranged for in the '40s."

Tucker went on to point out that Mulligan's foray into classical music was "symptomatic of the increasing fluidity in late-20th-century American musical life. It seems as if everyone is crossing over these days: Itzhak Perlman plays Hoagy Carmichael, the Kronos Quartet programs Monk and Jimi Hendrix, Linda Ronstadt sings Puccini, Keith Jarrett interprets Bach and Mozart, and the rock drummer Stewart Copeland writes grand opera. One result of this activity is a kind of ventilation of the concert hall; rather than a dusty museum devoted to past relics, it is slowly opening its doors to more contemporary currents.

"According to Mr. Mulligan," Tucker continued, "not just audiences but classical musicians appreciate the change. 'There's a lot of enthusiasm on the part of orchestras to play music that relates to jazz,' he says. 'Many of the younger players have had experience in dance and jazz bands. This familiarity with their own music has changed their attitude.'"

Mulligan's rhythm section for the Lincoln Center performance again included Johnson on bass, but for the New York performances, he was joined by Bill Charlap on piano and Rich DeRosa on drums. Noting that Mulligan had first appeared with the Philharmonic in 1982 as a surprise guest soloist on "Bolero," the program notes went on to point out that, while he was "best known as a baritone saxophonist," Mulligan, "has been active as a soloist, composer, arranger, and conductor since the 1940s . . ."

In preparation for the Lincoln Center performances with Mehta, Mulligan provided some commentary on both "Entente" and "K-4 Pacific" for the concerts' program notes, again written by Phillip Ramey. "According to the dictionary," Mulligan said, "an entente is an agreement or understanding. The agreement sought in this instance is between the diverse elements of the jazz-based baritone saxophone and the symphony orchestra. 'Entente' is a rhapsody that allows the soloist the option of an improvisational approach. The strings and winds are treated as separate timbral groups, doubling occurring between the two units at climactic passages only . . .

"'K-4 Pacific,'" he explained, "was the designation given to the fast and powerful locomotive that formerly drove the express trains of the Pennsylvania Railroad on the main line to Chicago. In my piece, the first section gradually builds in intensity, when, at full strength, the orchestra 'breaks' to allow solo statements by the baritone saxophone, the piano, the bass, and then the drums of the jazz quartet. The last section represents, with all the forces of the jazz quartet and the orchestra, the full dynamic power and velocity of the locomotive at top speed, and ends with its triumphal arrival at its destination."

At the end of the first Lincoln Center performance, according to Franca, "Zubin Mehta told Gerry that after he finished conducting 'K-4 Pacific,' he turned around and saw the audience in a standing ovation. He said to Gerry, 'I never saw those old ladies standing for any performance at Lincoln Center during the many years I have been at the New York Philharmonic, except for you.'"

While writing "Entente," Mulligan had begun creating a series of drawings, reflecting his various moods while composing. "When he was in Milano writing for the symphony orchestra," Franca revealed, "he would say, 'Franca, I need some paper. I want to draw.' And then he would take pen and pencil and draw on a yellow pad. Then, he said, 'Can we buy some real paper so I can draw better?' So, for six months, he did that, and we had one hundred seventy-five drawings. I kept them secret because I wanted to have an exhibition with Gerry's classical music." In March 2014, the Royal Academy of Fine Arts and the Royal Conservatory of Liege, Belgium, held a world-premiere exhibition of Mulligan's artwork in a program called "Jazz Meets Classic!" at which his artwork was shown along with concerts of his compositions for chamber orchestras, performed by the conservatory students.

In the late '80s and early '90s, Mulligan appeared with several other classical orchestras including the Stockholm Philharmonic, the Philadelphia Orchestra, and the Los Angeles Philharmonic. In April 1990, the Sea Cliff Chamber Players on New York's Long Island premiered another Mulligan classical work, "In Camera," for baritone saxophone and chamber ensemble. The program also included "Trout Quintet" by Schubert and "Septet in E-flat Major" by Beethoven. The front of the program said: "Schubert! Beethoven! Mulligan!" Inside were the startled faces of Schubert and Beethoven over the headline, "Mulligan?" And then below it to the right it said: "Yes . . .Gerry Mulligan!" with his photo.

The copy pointed out that, "In recent years, Mulligan has been appearing with major symphony orchestras, including the New York Philharmonic and the Boston 'Pops.' As a composer, he has developed an international reputation whose works have been performed in concert halls worldwide. Mulligan's new work, 'In Camera,' has been commissioned by the Sea Cliff Chamber Players, a nationally recognized ensemble of award-winning artists. What makes this program unique is not Mulligan, or Schubert, or Beethoven, but that these three composers are joined together by a universal musical impulse: Theme & Variations, a form so superbly realized by Schubert in the 'Trout' Quintet, the most popular chamber work of all time . . . by Beethoven, in the exquisite slow movement of his extraordinary 'Septet,' a chamber work of orchestral dimensions . . . and, particularly relevant in our own time as the soul of jazz improvisation."

Mulligan had heard a lot of classical composers when he was growing up. "My family loved the Victrola and loved to collect records," he said. "They loved show music and a lot of the lighter classics—Liszt and Chopin." But the real credit for his interest in and appreciation for classical music, he said, goes to Gene Krupa for carrying around that phonograph with classical records while the band was on the road.

In the 1974 interview with *Down Beat*'s Patricia Willard, Mulligan cautioned jazz musicians about how they approached jazz-classical combinations. "We must not let jazz duplicate the dilemma of symphonic music," he said. "Symphony composers got so busy writing for each other and assuming that their audience was square that they finally wrote themselves into a corner. Their music has become so complex that only composers can understand each other."

Raph, who was classically trained, said he has noticed that jazz musicians "hear much better than classical musicians. A classical musician, by and large—and there are many, many exceptions—plays extremely well, and the world revolves around his instrument. With a jazz musician, the world revolves around the music he's playing, and he hears what the other guy's doing. He adds to what the other guy's doing, and he relates to the other guy, and there's interplay. In classical music, when you hear a fine string quartet, there's interplay between the musicians, but it's always the same—the Juilliard String Quartet doing Beethoven one night is pretty much the same as the night before. Jazz is freer, more of a dialogue. There's more communication."

With Sarah Vaughan in 1979.

Backstage with Gil Evans at Avery Fisher Hall in 1982.

Gerry and Mel Tormé at Carnegie Hall in 1983.

Recording *2:00 AM Paradise Café* with Barry Manilow in 1984.

Antonio Carlos Jobim and Gerry became "great friends." They performed together at the Botanical Garden in Rio de Janeiro in 1986.

With, *from left to right*, Dave McKenna, Zoot Sims, and Al Cohn at Church of the Heavenly Rest in New York City, 1985.

"Entente" for Saxophone and Orchestra was first performed and Zubin Mehta with the Israel Philharmonic Orchestra in 1987.

THE ISRAEL PHILHARMONIC ORCHESTRA
Founded in 1936 by Bronislaw Huberman • Music Director: Zubin Mehta

התזמורת הפילהרמונית הישראלית
נוסדה בתרצ"ו 1936 בידי ברוניסלב הוברמן • מנהל מוסיקלי: זובין מהטה

Change of Programme: | **שינוי בתוכנית:**

Light Classical Music
Subscription Concert No. 6
Tel-Aviv, The Fredric R. Mann Auditorium
Saturday, 4 July 1987

מוסיקה קלאסית קלה
קונצרט למנויים מס׳ 6
תל־אביב, היכל התרבות ע״ש פרדריק ר׳ מאן
מוצ״ש, ד׳ בתמוז תשמ״ז, 4 ביולי 1987

Zubin Mehta
conductor
Itzhak Perlman
violinist
Gerry Mulligan
saxophonist

זוּבין מֶהְטָה
מנצח
יצחק פֶּרלמָן
כנר
ג׳רי מאליגן
נגן סאקסופון

FRANZ LISZT (1811–1886)
Hungarian Rhapsody no. 6
(First IPO Performance)

פראנץ ליסט (1886–1811)
רַפְּסוֹדְיָה הוּנגָרית מס׳ 6
(ביצוע ראשון בפילהרמונית)

DOV SELTZER (b. 1932)
Three Jewish Melodies
(Dedicated to Itzhak Perlman)
When the Rebbe Elimelech
A Yiddishe Mamme (A Jewish Mother)
Doyna
Itzhak Perlman, violinist
Israel Zohar, clarinetist

דב זֶלצֶר (נו׳ 1932)
שלוש נעימות יהודיות לכינור ולתזמורת
(מוקדש ליצחק פרלמן)
כְּשֶׁהָרֶבִּי אֱלִימֶלֶךְ
אם יהודיה (אַ יידישע מאמע)
דוֹינָה
יצחק פֶּרלמָן, כנר
ישראל זוהר, קלרניתן (כליזמר)

Intermission | הפסקה

GERRY MULLIGAN (b. 1927)
"Entente", for baritone-saxophone and orchestra (1984)
(First IPO Performance)

ג׳רי מאליגן (נו׳ 1927)
"הֲבָנָה הדדית" ("אַנְטאנְט")
לסאקסופון־באריטון ולתזמורת (1984)
(ביצוע ראשון בפילהרמונית)

GERRY MULLIGAN (b. 1927)
Jazz Selections
Gerry Mulligan and his Quartet
Gerry Mulligan, saxophonist
Harold Danko, pianist
Dean Douglas Johnson, bassist
Charles (Butch) Miles, drummer

ג׳רי מאליגן (נו׳ 1927)
קטעי ג׳ז
ג׳רי מאליגן ורביעייתו:
ג׳רי מאליגן, נגן סאקסופון
הארולד דאנקו, פסנתרן
דין דאגלס ג׳ונסון, נגן־באס
צ׳ארלז (בוץ׳) מיילס, מתופף

GERRY MULLIGAN (b. 1927)
"Pacific K-4" for jazz quartet and symphony orchestra
(First IPO Performance)
Gerry Mulligan and his Quartet
Gerry Mulligan, saxophonist
Harold Danko, pianist
Dean Douglas Johnson, bassist
Charles (Butch) Miles, drummer

ג׳רי מאליגן (נו׳ 1927)
"פאסיפיק ק־4" לרביעיית ג׳ז ולתזמורת סימפונית
(ביצוע ראשון בפילהרמונית)
ג׳רי מאליגן ורביעייתו:
ג׳רי מאליגן, נגן סאקסופון
הארולד דאנקו, פסנתרן
דין דאגלס ג׳ונסון, נגן־באס
צ׳ארלז (בוץ׳) מיילס, מתופף

BELOW: When Gerry came out for an encore after his performance with the Israel Philharmonic Orchestra, he was joined by Itzhak Perlman for a duet of Hoagy Carmichael's "Georgia on My Mind."

THE ISRAEL PHILHARMONIC ORCHESTRA
Founded in 1936 by Bronislaw Huberman • Music Director: Zubin Mehta
FESTIVE JUBILEE SEASON

התזמורת הפילהרמונית הישראלית
נוסדה בתרצ"ו / 1936 בידי ברוניסלב הוברמן • מנהל מוסיקלי: זובין מהטה
עונת היובל החגיגית

Zubin Mehta
conductor
Itzhak Perlman
violinist
Gerry Mulligan
saxophonist

זוּבין מֶהְטָה
מנצח
יצחק פֶּרלמָן
כנר
ג׳רי מאליגן
נגן סאקסופון

FRANZ LISZT (1811–1886)
Hungarian Rhapsody no. 6
(First IPO Performance)

פראנץ ליסט (1886–1811)
רַפְּסוֹדְיָה הוּנגָרית מס׳ 6
(ביצוע ראשון בפילהרמונית)

DOV SELTZER (b. 1932)
Three Jewish Melodies
(Dedicated to Itzhak Perlman)
When the Rebbe Elimelech
A Yiddishe Mamme (A Jewish Mother)
Doyna
Itzhak Perlman, violinist
Israel Zohar, clarinetist

דב זֶלצֶר (נו׳ 1932)
שלוש נעימות יהודיות לכינור ולתזמורת
(מוקדש ליצחק פֶּרלמָן)
כְּשֶׁהָרֶבִּי אֱלִימֶלֶךְ
אם יהודיה (אַ יידישע מאמע)
דוֹינָה
יצחק פֶּרלמָן, כנר
ישראל זוהר, קלרניתן (כליזמר)

Intermission | הפסקה

GERRY MULLIGAN (b. 1927)
"Entente", for baritone-saxophone and orchestra (1984)
(First IPO Performance)

ג׳רי מאליגן (נו׳ 1927)
"הֲבָנָה הדדית" ("אַנְטאנְט")
לסאקסופון־באריטון ולתזמורת (1984)
(ביצוע ראשון בפילהרמונית)

GERRY MULLIGAN (b. 1927)
Jazz Improvisations
Gerry Mulligan and his Quartet
Gerry Mulligan, saxophonist
Harold Danko, pianist
Dean Douglas Johnson, bassist
Charles (Butch) Miles, drummer

ג׳רי מאליגן (נו׳ 1927)
אילתורי ג׳ז
ג׳רי מאליגן ורביעייתו:
ג׳רי מאליגן, נגן סאקסופון
הארולד דאנקו, פסנתרן
דין דאגלס ג׳ונסון, נגן־באס
צ׳ארלז (בוץ׳) מיילס, מתופף

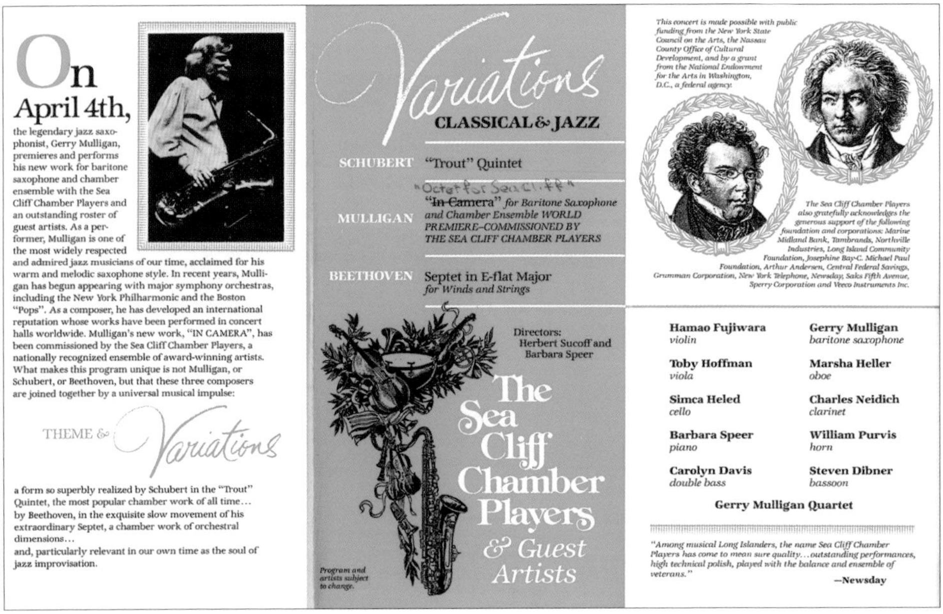

In April 1987, the Sea Cliff Chamber Players on New York's Long Island premiered Gerry Mulligan's classical work "In Camera."

Gerry and Franca at Lincoln Center in 1989 during the Gerry Mulligan Quartet's performances with the New York Philharmonic.

NEW YORK PHILHARMONIC

AVERY FISHER HALL
LINCOLN CENTER FOR
THE PERFORMING ARTS

ONE HUNDRED FORTY-EIGHTH SEASON 1989-90
ZUBIN MEHTA, *Music Director*
HOME OF THE NEW YORK PHILHARMONIC

Thursday Evening, December 14, 1989, at 8:00
Friday Afternoon, December 15, 1989, at 2:00
Saturday Evening, December 16, 1989, at 8:00
Tuesday Evening, December 19, 1989, at 8:00

11,452nd, 11,453rd, 11,455th and 11,456th Concerts

Zubin Mehta, *Conductor*

GERRY MULLIGAN, *Saxophonist*
THE GERRY MULLIGAN QUARTET
(New York Philharmonic Debut)
Bill Charlap, *Piano*
Dean Johnson, *Doublebass*
Richard De Rosa, *Drums*
Gerry Mulligan, *Saxophone*

BEETHOVEN Overture to "Fidelio"*

BEETHOVEN Symphony No. 4, B-flat major, Opus 60*
I Adagio; Allegro vivace
II Adagio
III Menuetto: Allegro vivace
IV Allegro ma non troppo

Intermission

MULLIGAN "Entente" for Baritone Saxophone and Orchestra

Works by the Gerry Mulligan Quartet

MULLIGAN "K-4 Pacific"

*Recorded by the New York Philharmonic and currently available.

Program from the 1989 performances with the New York Philharmonic.

Performing with Zubin Mehta at a Young People's Concert in 1989.

Gerry Mulligan Quartet performing with the New York Philharmonic, conducted by Zubin Mehta, 1989.

The rhythm section for the New York Philharmonic concert. *From left*: pianist Bill Charlap, bassist Dean Johnson, and drummer Rich DeRosa.

With Bob Brookmeyer and Dean Johnson in Rotterdam, 1991.

"When Dave Grusin plays my tunes, I always learn something new," Mulligan said. Grusin, *at right*, with Mulligan during the recording of Gerry's last album, *Dragonfly*.

Greeting Bill and Hillary Clinton at the Kennedy Center Honors ceremony in 1995.

Program from Gerry Mulligan's memorial service at Saint Peter's Church in New York City, on February 12, 1996.

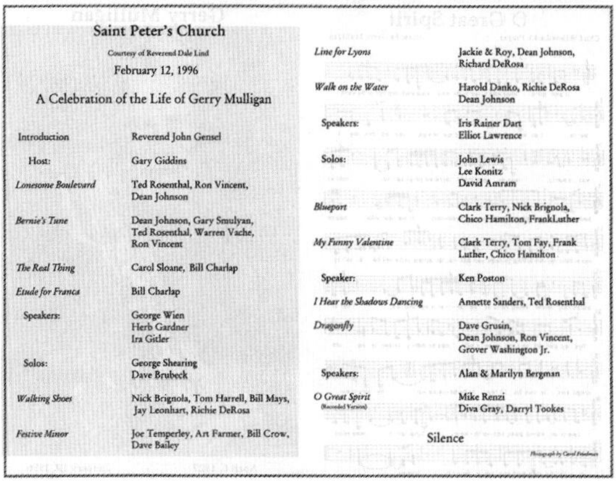

Saint Peter's Church

Courtesy of Reverend Dale Lind

February 12, 1996

A Celebration of the Life of Gerry Mulligan

Introduction	Reverend John Gensel
Host:	Gary Giddins
Lonesome Boulevard	Ted Rosenthal, Ron Vincent, Dean Johnson
Bernie's Tune	Dean Johnson, Gary Smulyan, Ted Rosenthal, Warren Vache, Ron Vincent
The Real Thing	Carol Sloane, Bill Charlap
Etude for Franca	Bill Charlap
Speakers:	George Wien Herb Gardner Ira Gitler
Solos:	George Shearing Dave Brubeck
Walking Shoes	Nick Brignola, Tom Harrell, Bill Mays, Jay Leonhart, Richie DeRosa
Festive Minor	Joe Temperley, Art Farmer, Bill Crow, Dave Bailey

Line for Lyons	Jackie & Roy, Dean Johnson, Richard DeRosa
Walk on the Water	Harold Danko, Richie DeRosa Dean Johnson
Speakers:	Iris Rainer Dart Elliot Lawrence
Solos:	John Lewis Lee Konitz David Amram
Blueport	Clark Terry, Nick Brignola, Chico Hamilton, FrankLuther
My Funny Valentine	Clark Terry, Tom Fay, Frank Luther, Chico Hamilton
Speaker:	Ken Poston
I Hear the Shadows Dancing	Annette Sanders, Ted Rosenthal
Dragonfly	Dave Grusin, Dean Johnson, Ron Vincent, Grover Washington Jr.
Speakers:	Alan & Marilyn Bergman
O Great Spirit (Recorded Version)	Mike Renzi Diva Gray, Darryl Tookes

Silence

Photograph by Carol Friedman

The 1997 Gerry Mulligan All-Star Tribute Band, *clockwise from far left*: Ron Vincent, Lee Konitz, Ted Rosenthal, Randy Brecker, Dean Johnson, and Bob Brookmeyer.

Opening ceremony for the presentation of the Gerry Mulligan Collection to the Library of Congress, 1999.

This photograph is featured in the same display case as Gerry Mulligan's gold-plated baritone saxophone, part of the permanent exhibition dedicated to Gerry Mulligan in the foyer of the Performing Arts Reading Room of the Library of Congress. Photo by Caspari De Geus, 1992.

14

'HE HEARD EVERY PART IN HIS HEAD'

In July 1991, Miles Davis and Quincy Jones assembled an orchestra at the Montreux Jazz Festival to re-create some of the music Davis had recorded with Gil Evans, who died in 1988. The performance was recorded and released as *Miles & Quincy Live at Montreux* by Warner Bros. Records in 1993. It featured one selection from the original *Birth of the Cool* recording, "Boplicity," cowritten by Evans and Davis and arranged by Evans.

A couple of weeks after the Montreux concert, Mulligan talked to Davis about participating in a "Re-Birth of the Cool" project. "He was pleased about it," Mulligan said. "Later on, I talked to him on the phone, and he didn't feel quite as enthusiastic about it, but he said to let him know because he might do it with me. About the time I was going to get in touch with him, he started having strokes, and that was the end of it. He died not long after that." (Miles Davis died on September 28, 1991, at St. John's Hospital and Health Center in Santa Monica, California. Cause of death was pneumonia, respiratory failure, and a stroke. He was sixty-five.)

"It would have been interesting to try to do something with him," Mulligan reflected, "because he and I hadn't done anything for years." The natural choice to play Davis's trumpet part for the new project was Wallace Roney, a protégé of Davis's who had performed at the Montreux concert. "I had been following Miles around and hanging with him since 1983," Roney told me. "He was my idol since I was a kid. He told me he looked in the mirror, and he saw Gil in the mirror, and Gil said, 'You got to go back and play this stuff.' After Montreux, he was so happy about it, and he said, 'Me and Quincy are talking about taking it on the road.'

"Then, Gerry Mulligan asked him about doing 'Re-Birth of the Cool.' Now, I didn't think he would do that, but he said yes. A month later, he got sick and passed. When Gerry called me and said Miles had agreed to do this, I had already known. We got together to rehearse, and it was really funny, because we played 'Boplicity.' Miles had taught me this way of playing. I didn't play it the way it was written. I played it the way Miles taught me to phrase it. And Gerry was amazed. He said, 'How did you know that?' and I looked up to the sky and said 'Thanks' to Miles. Miles had told me that he loved Gerry."

Two members of the original *BOTC* nonet, in addition to Mulligan—pianist John Lewis and tubist Bill Barber—were available for the new album, *Re-Birth of the Cool*, recorded and released in 1992 on GRP Records. Lee Konitz was unavailable and was replaced on alto saxophone by Phil Woods. The remaining band members were: Dave Bargeron, trombone; John Clark, French horn; Dean Johnson, bass; and Ron Vincent, drums. Mel Tormé replaced Kenny Hagood on the vocal for "Darn That Dream."

"It's interesting how an arrangement changes with different people playing it," Mulligan said. "So there are different values that came out of it, but I was pleased."

When Mulligan decided to approach Woods as a replacement for Konitz, some fence mending was necessary. Mulligan had been artistic director of the Ravinia Festival in Chicago a couple of years earlier, and, according to Woods, "we had a big fight there. When I brought my quintet there, I did not do a sound check, and he told me how unprofessional I was. We played there every year. We knew the soundmen; they knew how we worked. So when Gerry called me to do *Re-Birth of the Cool*, I said, 'Well, why would you want such an unprofessional man as me?' He apologized."

In an article in *Saxophone Journal*, written a few months after Mulligan's death, Woods talked about the experience of making the *Re-Birth* recording. "Working on that album," he said, "was a delight. I grew up with those sounds and felt honored to take part. Gerry knew exactly what he wanted on this album and communicated his wishes succinctly and directly. Oh, what a better workplace it would be if all leaders had such a handle on a project."

Roney described Mulligan as "brilliant. I learned some very cool things about him. My heroes were Miles Davis, John Coltrane, Red Garland, Herbie Hancock, Tony Williams, Wayne Shorter, Charlie Parker, Dizzy Gillespie, Ornette Coleman. These were my heroes—geniuses. I added Gerry Mulligan to this list because I saw him display his genius. I saw him take an arrangement, tear it apart, and redo it right there. He heard every part in his head. He would reorchestrate it—not just the notes, but the moving lines. I said, 'This man can hear.'

"And his baritone playing! He was a wonderful baritone saxophone player. We talk about Pepper Adams. But Gerry Mulligan was maybe better. Gerry Mulligan was something else because of his knowledge of harmony and orchestration. He was just about the music; the music was the key. He could be a taskmaster, but he was only doing it to serve the music."

The *Re-Birth of the Cool* album was coproduced by Mulligan and John Snyder, who is now chair of the Music Industry Studies program at Loyola University in New Orleans. Trombonist Dave Bargeron knew Snyder from his association with Gil Evans's band. "I was really looking forward to playing with all these guys," Bargeron told me. "Since we were going to do it over a three-day period, there was going to be a lot of conversation and hang time. I just couldn't wait.

"During the recording," Bargeron continued, "Gerry was very exacting. This guy was a great musician. He knew what he wanted, and he knew he could get it from these people. So all he did was to be very articulate about how he wanted certain things and hearkened back to the way they were done in the first place."

A major difference between the original recording and the *Re-Birth* recording, Bargeron pointed out, was the advancement of recording technology. In the original sessions, he explained, "you had a band full of nine different instruments. And the arrangements were so good that they were written to blend well. You heard the blend, but you couldn't really discern different instruments like you would if you went to a nightclub where you could hear it all blend but hear everybody individually, too. With modern technology, you could do that by 1991. I think that was a big reason for redoing the record. A lot of the original sessions were audibly a blur compared to what we were clearly able to put down because of the new recording technology. Same notes. Same arrangements. Same intent.

Clearer. That was the point." AllMusic's Scott Yanow noted this, saying, "It is a particular pleasure to listen to them [the original arrangements] with the improved recording quality." And *Down Beat*'s Kevin Whitehead, in August 1992, said: "It's good that we can hear the parts more clearly."

For Bargeron, "just to be taking the place of J. J. Johnson and Kai Winding was quite an honor for me. And Wallace Roney was a perfect choice for those sessions. He had a very close association with Miles, and he's only one of two people in my lifetime who really could capture—and does capture—the sound of Miles's instrument and the intent of a lot of his music. There's another guy in Denmark, but I've forgotten his name. He could do it, too—get close to a kind of imitation and still have a creative pride of his own. That's pretty amazing, really. It's very rare to able to do that."

Drummer Ron Vincent recalled that when Mulligan first contacted him about the project, "he had told me Miles was interested in coming and doing it, and I had my fingers crossed big time for that one." The assignment was a little intimidating for Vincent because "I'd grown up listening to that record. Here I was, recording with John Lewis and Bill Barber, the original tuba player. And Phil Woods doing the record because Lee was busy. Here are all these big stars. I am truly happy I was able to do that record. I was in the right place at the right time."

Roney enjoyed the opportunity to play with Lewis. "On 'Rouge,' I'd take a solo, and we just started interacting. We were playing off of each other. He would just look at me and smile. I had good rapport with him, we bonded."

The original *Birth of the Cool* group started off as a rehearsal band, played a few club dates, and made the historic recording. But, Mulligan reflected, "We never worked in a concert setting." After the *Re-Birth* recording, he decided to add a second trumpet and a second baritone saxophone and take the band out on the road as a "tentette" (actually eleven pieces). "I was anxious to see how it worked," he said. "I wanted to change the structure of the arrangements to adapt them to more soloists. I felt the *Birth of the Cool* instrumentation was a little weak for a concert, especially festivals where we played. Having the 'tentette' setup with the second trumpet and an extra baritone gave enough extra guts to it to feel a little more at home in these big settings. It was a totally acoustical ensemble. The whole was based on the blend we could get between the instruments. It was, for me, a very important learning experience."

The "tentette" toured for seven months, January to July 1992. Roney wasn't part of the tour because he had joined the VSOP quintet with Herbie Hancock, Ron Carter, Tony Williams, and Wayne Shorter. So the Miles Davis trumpet role was taken over by Art Farmer, who had played with Mulligan's pianoless quartet in the late '50s.

In June 1992, the band appeared at Carnegie Hall, prior to a European tour, as part of the JVC Jazz Festival. For this appearance, Lee Konitz joined the group on alto sax. Jon Pareles, reviewing the concert for *The New York Times*, pointed out that "Mr. Mulligan followed an established jazz-repertory approach. He used the original arrangements and tempos while adding new solos, some of them variants on the recorded ones . . . Mr. Mulligan and Mr. Konitz were both in fine form, Mr. Mulligan gruff and swaggering on baritone saxophone, Mr. Konitz leisurely and oblique on alto."

In the mid-'90s, Mulligan once again toured with Brubeck. This time, instead of Mulligan playing with Brubeck's trio, it was the Gerry Mulligan Quartet and the Dave Brubeck Quartet sharing the bill, with the two stars coming out at the end to play together. Ted Rosenthal has wonderful memories of those tours. "The Gerry Mulligan Quartet partnering up with the Dave Brubeck Quartet—that was really special," he said. "We got to play in many great halls in Europe and to go to Japan, but we also got to spend some time with Brubeck and get a feel for his whole world."

The connection between Mulligan and Brubeck continued to be very close. "Gerry," Franca Mulligan said, "felt the Brubecks were like a kind of family, which he never had. He had a great relationship with Dave's children. He felt their affection. When Gerry went on tour with Dave, it was wonderful. No competition, no egos. It was always fun to be together, a joy. They were two great people—Dave and Iola, really special, and very spiritual."

15

'KINGS OF THE BARITONE SAX'

Gerry Mulligan, by all accounts, was accepted by veteran jazz musicians at a very early age, had great reverence for the music's history, and served as a mentor for the young musicians who joined his bands in the last three decades of his life.

Sprinkled throughout his recorded autobiography are personal comments about some of the music legends he encountered and played with throughout his career. This chapter is a gathering of some of those reflections.

Duke Ellington. "In 1954 or '55, Duke Ellington and Billy Strayhorn had written a piece for Harry Carney and me. I loved doing it with them. I was around the band a lot and around Duke a lot. We traveled together on those shows [Jazz at the Philharmonic] for four or five years. By that time, we were old friends. I had great feelings and respect for him. I loved his approach to music. Duke always introduced me as the world's second-best baritone player, and Harry and I became great friends. We wound up in Japan at the time, and Harry and I hung out in Tokyo for days. What a gentle, smart man he was."

The piece that Ellington and Strayhorn wrote for Mulligan and Carney was "Prima Bara Dubla." It was performed at the Newport Jazz Festival in July 1958 by the Duke Ellington Orchestra with Mulligan as the guest soloist. In the liner notes for the resulting album, *Newport 1958*, Irving Townsend pointed out that "The highlight of the concert was when the kings of the baritone sax, Gerry Mulligan and Harry Carney, stood in the limelight . . ."

"Duke, every once in a while," Mulligan pointed out, "would make an album of pop tunes, and his arrangements of some of these tunes would always have a twist to them—he would find an eccentric quality to the tune, or he could find some kind of hook. Some of those things, I'd really like to do. They were kind of a lesson in how to look at things. It's how to see something fresh in something that's really kind of trite."

Stan Getz. "Charlie Ventura decided to leave the Gene Krupa band. So, Gene needed a replacement. I had heard the record of Randy Brooks's band that Stan Getz played on, and he just sounded terrific. He really sounded wonderful. So I immediately started trying to talk Gene into getting a hold of Stan. The arrangers often used saxophone solos like cadenzas for key changes. The book was really based around featuring the tenor. Gene did get a hold of Stan and invited him to join the band. They went out and played a one-nighter, and the guys in the band told me Stan was really great.

"One day, after one of those performances, I was walking into Charlie's Tavern (a musicians' hangout in midtown New York City), really pleased that he was going to join, and Stan Getz is walking out. I said, 'Stan, so glad,' and, before I got anything out of my mouth, he said, 'If you want to keep living, keep walking. I know you went with my old lady before I married her,' and took off. That kind of colored my relationship for all the years I knew Stan. I'd see him, and he would be insulting or insufferable. The next time I'd see him, he'd either be apologetic or just go along as if nothing had happened. He was absolutely mercurial. He would pull the dumbest things. I never could understand it. I never could trust him. I never knew what to expect.

"After Zoot died, I was asked to play at a jazz festival in Chicago. They had [Jimmy] Giuffre and Stan. They wanted us to play the 'Four Brothers' [sax section from Woody Herman's bands], and they wanted me to do a few numbers with Stan's rhythm section, who were playing for this whole segment. I told the agent, 'I'd like to do that for Zoot's tribute, but I don't think playing with Stan's rhythm section is a good idea. I think it's going to create a problem.' I finally said I would do it, but I wanted the agent's assurance that I would have a rehearsal and that they were agreeable that they knew they were going to play with me. He said, 'Fine, we'll cover all that.'

"So, the day of the concert I show up for rehearsal, and the rhythm section comes in fit to be tied. They're furious. They had gotten in from someplace at nine o'clock in the morning after a long trip, and they didn't know about the rehearsal. Of course, the agent didn't talk directly with the musicians; he talked to Stan. I could see Stan's fine hand at work. They were very hostile. I had to take them aside, one at a time, and explain that I thought they had known about the rehearsal. I also told them I was going to pay them extra for playing with me, so the guys cooled it, and when we did the show that night, they were great. Stan was fit to be tied. He was furious that the guys were playing well for me. I just laughed—finally I was able to give something back at him that he had laid on me all these years. I had upset his whole plan because obviously he had planned this whole thing to make a scene.

"Stan was kind of peculiar, and he didn't seem to give a damn about what anybody thought of him. It was like he went out of his way to alienate people. I had some times with him that were great musically and personally, but I never knew what to expect."

Woody Herman. "I thought Woody was a wonderful man. I liked the way Woody played. He expressed himself and was effective. There was a quality about the players in the '47 band that they were so full of themselves, and [baritone saxophonist] Serge Chaloff was greatly responsible for this. They made life miserable for [arranger] Ralph Burns because he was influenced by Duke Ellington. Serge and the rest of them thought if it wasn't Count Basie, it didn't swing. Serge could be really cruel. He would ridicule Woody's playing on the stand. I was kind of mad at Woody for putting up with it, but Woody appreciated good musicians so much that he took a lot of crap from them."

Antonio Carlos Jobim. "I met Jobim, João Gilberto, and Sergio Mendes at Carnegie Hall when they first came to New York in 1962 or '63. When I went into the dressing room, Tom [Jobim] and João were there. They took one look at me, and João sang the song from 'Bernie's

Tune' from beginning to end. They knew very well all of the stuff I had done with the quartet, tentette, *Birth of the Cool* stuff. And Jobim and I became great friends.

"There was one time when Jobim and I were at Judy [Holliday]'s apartment together in the Dakota, taking turns playing the piano. He'd play something he wrote, and I'd play something I wrote. Judy would start laughing. She'd say, 'I'm the Russian Jew. I'm supposed to be sad, but you guys—a Brazilian/Portuguese fisherman and this Irishman—each piece that you play is a little sadder than the one before.'"

Charles Mingus. "When Charlie was dying of ALS, Franca and I had told him about this healer in Mexico, so the last time I saw him, he and Susan [his wife] were packing to go off to Mexico. It was an awkward thing because we knew it was the last time we'd see each other. We were waiting for an elevator. Charlie's sitting in a wheelchair. He backs himself into the elevator. We're in there looking at each other. The elevator starts going up. It struck us both at the same time. We started laughing. It was right out of a movie. The elevator's taking him to heaven. We just roared. And that's the last time I saw Charlie. We left each other laughing. He was a good man. I liked him very much."

Thelonius Monk. "Thelonius and I were pals. We only lived a few blocks away from each other and spent a lot of time together. Oddly enough, we never played together. We always hung out at each other's place, talking about writing, ideas we had for orchestration, etc. And I spent a lot time transcribing his tunes that weren't written down. Monk had a date with Riverside. They wanted to record the quartet he was playing in with John Coltrane at the Half Note. But Coltrane was tied up in a contract with somebody else and they couldn't get a release for him to play. So they were kind of stuck. I guess they were thinking Thelonius would make a trio album when they found out that Thelonius and I were friends. They said, 'Do you think Gerry would record something with you?' and Monk said, 'Sure he would.' So that's how that [*Mulligan Meets Monk*] came about. I felt like I was walking on a tightrope because, not having ever played together, I was feeling my way. The way that Monk accompanies you and the way he approaches chord progressions really demanded a whole different melodic approach for me. That turned out to be the only time we recorded together, kind of a happy accident."

Mulligan Meets Monk, originally recorded in 1957, was reissued in 2010 by Hallmark and in 2013 by Original Jazz Classics. Reviewing one of the reissues on AllMusic, Anthony Tognazzini wrote that Mulligan and Monk "sound remarkable together . . . the contrast between the players' styles lends this set its balance and appeal . . . great tunes, chemistry, and soloing—a true classic."

"Monk loved Gerry," said David Amram. "Otherwise, they wouldn't have made that record together. And Gerry loved working with Monk. Monk had such a great individual approach and a great sense of harmony. That was a fabulous record."

Two years earlier, Mulligan and Monk had performed together, along with Miles Davis, at the Newport Jazz Festival. George Wein re-created that moment for me. "Gerry was in that famous set with Monk and Miles at Newport," he recalled. "That was an amazing time in jazz, 1955, at the height of the time all these people were emerging as stars. None of them had a band—Monk, Mulligan, Miles. I had put together this set with Gerry, and Miles wasn't even on it. Miles met me one night in a club and said, 'You doing Newport? You can't do Newport without me.' I said I had one set with Monk and Mulligan. And the bass and drums were Percy Heath and Connie Kay. I said, 'You're going to play with an all-star group.' Of course, they made jazz history. That's when Miles played 'Round Midnight' and was signed by Columbia." The group also included Zoot Sims on tenor saxophone and is considered as a key moment in Davis's comeback, after recovering from addiction to heroin in the early 1950s.

Charlie Parker and Dizzy Gillespie. "When Bird played, it was like a new country had been heard from. It just was an altogether different atmosphere. And it was really striking because he played with such clarity. And then when the 'Quintet' record came out"—the recording of the May 15, 1953 Jazz at Massey Hall concert in Toronto with Parker, Dizzy Gillespie, Bud Powell, Max Roach and Charles Mingus—"it was very accessible to everybody.

"Bird and Diz were two quite separate entities, who, until they played together in Dizzy's small group, had very little to do with each other.

But in the context of the quintet, they were Dizzy's tunes and Dizzy's arrangements. They were good and made it kind of a showcase for Bird. It was wonderful, some of the best things that Bird ever recorded. Dizzy always had a very good sense of arranging. That was where he was coming from. He was really a band man and an arranger and a Roy Eldridge–influenced trumpet player. Bird was just something else altogether. He would take his melodic lines and run in a different meter. He would sail through this progression. He had an incredible facility, and the way he used a horn was marvelous. Bird was unique.

"It was Dizzy's interest in Cuban music that wound up combining elements of Cuban music with jazz. This was because of some of the musicians that Dizzy met—Chano Pozo and some of the other conga drum players. Some of those men were really dynamic players. In Dizzy's hands, they produced a very vital influence, a subgenre of jazz."

Bud Powell. "Bud Powell and I always had a special relationship. He felt a connection with me. It was kind of a mystical, spiritual thing. A lot of the times, he would seem so out of it, but when I was around, he would be very lucid."

Lester Young and Charlie Parker. "I'll never forget one time I was standing outside Birdland, and I see Prez's porkpie hat kind of sailing up the stairs—big grin, effortlessly. He kind of floated up the stairs. Right behind him, a couple of minutes later, came Charlie. And Charlie was stomping up the steps, so that the whole place rattled. Such a total difference of personalities."

Danny Polo. Clarinetist Polo couldn't be part of *Birth of the Cool* because he was on the road with Claude Thornhill, but Mulligan had great admiration for his playing. Polo, Mulligan said, "had absorbed a whole other style of playing [clarinet]. He wasn't playing bebop clarinet, but he was playing with an understanding of what had happened. I never really thought of myself as a bebop player and was criticized for that. Danny didn't imitate what was going on, but he absorbed it. He had a feeling and an understanding of what was going on. At that time [in the late 1940s], the clarinet became the forgotten instrument. Buddy DeFranco was a wonderful player, but Buddy was from another school. He was from the Benny Goodman school, but had also encompassed what Bird had done. What Danny did didn't have the angularity of bebop, but it fit the idiom perfectly."

Zoot Sims. "When Zoot finally came to New York, we immediately became good friends. Some of his California habits were a little hard for me to adjust to. He'd have chili dogs for breakfast."

Serge Chaloff. "At one point, I said, 'Serge, you've been winning the *Down Beat* poll [on baritone saxophone]. I'm going to give you two more years, and then I'm going to take it away from you. You've had it. And, by God, in two years, I started winning the poll. And Serge never got it back." (Mulligan won the *Down Beat* Readers Poll on Baritone Sax for forty-two consecutive years, from 1953 to 1995.)

Barry Manilow. "A number of times in interviews that I had heard and read, Barry said he was a fan of mine, and his stepfather had taken him to some place that I was playing when he was a kid. Finally, somebody introduced us. We became great friends. He was a very serious musician. He had a project that he had wanted to do (*2:00 AM Paradise Café*). It was kind of made to order for him to have me on it. He was playing piano, and Bill Mays was playing piano. Shelly Manne was on drums, and George Duvivier was on bass. He also had Mel Tormé and Sarah Vaughan as guests. He was great to watch in the studio because he knew what he wanted, and even with all those powerhouse players, who he was in awe of, he got them to do what he wanted them to do. He was a professional in the best sense of the term. It was a pleasure doing the album. I liked it very much. I did a couple of other projects with him, including one television thing that was fun to do."

The album consisted of original songs written by Manilow. In a review on AllMusic, Johnny Loftus wrote that Manilow was "able to sell the concept that this is all taking place in the wee hours inside a half-empty basement cabaret. The shuffling percussion of Shelly Manne is spot on, as are the cool tones of baritone sax man Gerry Mulligan—you can just picture the blinking neon from the hotel across the street reflecting in the gold of his horn." The television project to which Mulligan referred was *Big Fun on Swing Street*, a 1988 CBS TV special that also featured guitarist Stanley Clarke, vocalists Carmen McRae and Diane Schuur, and tenor saxophonist Tom Scott. In a review for Amazon, Tom Keogh pointed out that Manilow was "quite generous toward his guests, making sure they [got] to play some serious jazz."

Manilow, interviewed in the *Listen: Gerry Mulligan* video, said he had "always known that there was something special about this guy. He played like he was singing or something. With a big piece of plumbing, he was playing effortlessly."

Scott Hamilton. In 1986, Carl Jefferson, founder and president of Concord Jazz label, proposed that Mulligan record an album with young tenor saxophonist Scott Hamilton. "It was a project I wanted to do because I had heard Scotty Hamilton play, and it was obvious to me that his heroes as tenor players were the guys that I liked so much," Mulligan said. "You could hear Zoot in his playing and Ben [Webster]. I wrote a bunch of stuff for it. He's a very talented player, and the album came out well." The album, *Scott Hamilton Meets Gerry Mulligan: Soft Lights & Sweet Music*, includes five Mulligan originals. The title track was written by Irving Berlin.

Alec Wilder. In a July 1973 "Jazz Salute to the American Song" at Lincoln Center's Philharmonic Hall, Mulligan and pianist Marian McPartland performed a tribute to the composer Alec Wilder that served as an inspiration for McPartland's 1974 Halcyon album *Marian McPartland Plays the Music of Alec Wilder*.

"Alec became a good friend," Mulligan said, "because, for a long time, instead of keeping an apartment in New York, I would live at the Algonquin Hotel. It had to do with my feelings about history. I was always fascinated with the place, the people of *The New Yorker* who made it their headquarters—Robert Benchley, Dorothy Parker. Alec always lived there. He was kind of a transient in life. He wasn't really interested in having a house or a home. He liked living in a hotel and then, when he was tired of that, he liked riding on a train to wherever he was going, and then he would get on another train. He would spend weeks traveling around on trains. I was fascinated by him. His face was kind of ravaged with life. Also,

I think he had gone through years of heavy drinking. We used to spend a lot of time together, and then as it turns out, later on, he was a great friend of Judy Holliday's.

"He wanted to write a piece for a woodwind quintet. One of his favorite people was John Barrows, the French horn player. So, he wanted to do it with the two solo horns—the French horn and me. As it turned out, John got sick or injured or something and wasn't able to play, so we never did the thing together. I always meant to bring it up to Gunther Schuller because he has a lot of Alec's music in his publishing company."

In the liner notes to McPartland's album, Bill Milkowski recalled the Lincoln Center concert. Mulligan and McPartland, accompanied by bassist Rusty Gilder and drummer Erroll Haywood, had opened with Wilder's "It's So Peaceful in the Country," followed by "While We're Young," which, Milkowski said, "serves as a springboard for some of Mulligan's most potent soloing of the concert." They concluded with "I'll Be Around," which was later featured on Mulligan's 1994 Telarc album *Dream a Little Dream*.

16

'A BARITONE SAXOPHONE SOUNDING LIKE A CELLO'

Gerry Mulligan characterized his switch to baritone saxophone in the '40s as "one of those left-field decisions. It seemed like a pretty arbitrary thing to do." Little did he realize the impact that choice would have on the instrument's future.

"Up until Gerry," said Bill Crow, "Harry Carney was the sound everyone heard when they thought of the baritone saxophone. Pepper Adams made his mark in there somewhere, but Gerry really changed the way people thought about it. I remember when Stan Kenton first started to record. He was the one who had the baritone saxophone doubling the melody on the bottom of the section. Duke had never done that; he always had Harry up in the high register.

"When Gerry came along and developed the quartet sound he had, when he played behind other soloists, he played what maybe a whole saxophone section would be playing. He figured out a way to make those little riffs and harmonies fit."

Before Mulligan, said Phil Woods, "it was Harry Carney. Gerry lightened up the whole thing. He freed up that upper register, which was so lovely, giving it a kind of a tenor sound." That tenor sound reflected the influence on Mulligan of Lester Young. To pianist Harold Danko, Mulligan "played a lot like Lester Young. He loved Lester. He tried and succeeded at sounding effortless. And I think that was what he wanted. I think he used the word 'fly.' That was a Lester Young term. He wanted it to be 'fly,' kind of effortless." Ted Hogarth, the baritone saxophonist who has formed a Mulligan Mosaic big band in Chicago to preserve and play Mulligan's music, was first drawn to Mulligan's playing because "he had such wonderful facility and technique on the horn, but he wasn't flashy. Some people have great technique, and I hear them play, but that's all I hear. His improvisations are just so creative. Listening to him improvise, it's obvious to me that he's a composer. Some people I hear improvise, and they're very creative, but I don't hear that level of composition that Gerry has."

In bassist Dean Johnson's opinion, Mulligan is probably "the only baritone player who plays what people would consider a nice sound. Everyone got caught up in the growl of Pepper Adams. Gerry made the baritone tolerable to the regular audience. Guys who pick up the baritone now try for that harsher sound. Gerry would blend that sound in the way he would do a lot of horn lines behind the rhythm section. It's like a cello."

Pianist Bill Charlap agreed that Mulligan's playing was "a baritone saxophone sounding like a cello. He was what a jazz musician should be, which is an original. Nobody had a sound like that, although he was certainly influenced by Harry Carney and Lester Young. Gerry was an arranger and composer and saxophonist and improviser. He was all of those things. And all of them are part of the tapestry that made him who he was."

Gary Smulyan, considered one of the top baritone saxophonists playing today, feels, "It is impossible to play the baritone saxophone and not be influenced in one way, shape, or form by Gerry Mulligan. He was such a dominant force on the instrument."

In 1998, Smulyan joined with two other baritone saxophonists, Ronnie Cuber and Nick Brignola, to record an album on the Dreyfus label called *Three Baritone Saxophone Band Plays Mulligan*. It included several tunes closely associated with Mulligan, such as "Blue Port," "Black Nightgown," "Line for Lyons," and "Walkin' Shoes." "Playing those tunes again," Smulyan said, "you get another deep appreciation for how incredible his craft was as a composer. He had a really deep harmonic acuity."

Jazz Times's Josef Woodward felt the album was not only a "unique new project," but also: "True to the influence of the late Gerry Mulligan, who brought the instrument to a new plateau of public acclaim, they play without piano, allowing both freedom and challenge."

The baritone, Brignola told Woodward, "when played in the traditional way, always sounds like the buffoon of the saxophone family. If you think about it, a lot of the big-band charts written to feature the baritone have these funny noises that the baritone can make. They take advantage of the low range, the bottom . . . Mulligan actually proved that you didn't have to play that way. He had his own sound. It certainly wasn't a baritone section sound, like Harry Carney's."

Smulyan told Woodward that Mulligan "has a big impact on anybody who plays the baritone, if not directly, indirectly . . . You can't help not be touched by somebody who was such a monumental figure on the instrument. I have only the greatest admiration for his artistry. Just through the fact that I play the baritone, I'm influenced by him. I just don't think you can help it. It's just like anybody who plays the saxophone can't help but be influenced by Bird in some way."

Even before she started playing baritone saxophone, Lisa Parrott was drawn to the *Village Vanguard* Concert Jazz Band album. "When I moved to Sydney and went to college," she told me, "my teacher insisted that I should try the bari. He said he could hear me sounding good on that. So I feel like, more than anyone else, I really identify with Gerry Mulligan's way of playing the baritone. He was really the first guy I was aware of who really grabbed me as a bari player. My first experience of hearing him was with a big band. It just blew me away.

"It wasn't until many, many years later that I started playing some of his tunes. But what differentiates him from other bari players is his melodic approach. He's very much about melody. Even when he's playing bebop lines, he is incredibly melodic. You could tell that he was really hearing what he was playing." Parrott is the baritone saxophonist in the DIVA Jazz Orchestra, a mainstream all-female big band, led by drummer Sherrie Maricle.

"Every baritone player has checked out Gerry Mulligan," said Lauren Sevian, who currently tours with the Count Basie Orchestra and was a member of the Mingus Big Band that won a Grammy for *Live at the Jazz Standard* in 2011. She added, "He was definitely an influence on me. I feel like he made the baritone saxophone a household name. Initially, Pepper Adams attracted me. I liked Gerry's sound—it's not my sound, but I definitely transcribed it and tried to get some of that in my language. My freshman year at school [at the Manhattan School of Music], for a month, all I did was listen to Gerry Mulligan. I couldn't get enough of his sound on *Birth of the Cool.* I remember listening over and over to 'Venus de Milo.' His sound just lent itself to that configuration."

Claire Daly, six-time winner of the *Down Beat* Critics Poll for "Talent Deserving of Wider Recognition," didn't play baritone sax until she was in her twenties. "I was already working in New York as an alto player," she said, "and someone was selling a baritone. I played a note on it, and it was an epiphany. The range of the sound resonated to me in a very personal way. Gerry Mulligan's melodicism always appealed to me. I hope that I'm influenced by his beautiful sense of melody."

Baritone saxophonist Leigh Pilzer, a member of the Smithsonian Jazz Masterworks Orchestra, was admittedly more influenced by Adams than by Mulligan as a player. But Mulligan's impact on her, she said, would be "counterpoint and real awareness of what another instrumental player is doing. I really appreciate Mulligan's sensibility and interactivity."

Multi-reedist Scott Robinson feels he was more influenced on baritone by Carney and Leo Parks than by Mulligan, but "Mulligan just emphasized the solo nature of the instrument to such a great degree. He did more in that area than those other players did. He brought the baritone forward as a real solo instrument because of his melodic sense."

Robinson was selected to play baritone saxophone at a celebration on April 6, 1999, of the Library of Congress's acquisition of the Gerry Mulligan Collection, which has become a permanent exhibition in the Performing Arts Reading Room. The other musicians in the band, led by Bob Brookmeyer, were trumpeter Randy Brecker, alto saxophonist Dick Oatts, and Mulligan's last rhythm section of Ted Rosenthal on piano, Dean Johnson on bass, and Ron Vincent on drums.

"There were two components to the Library of Congress event," Robinson recalled. "The first was a ceremony for the dedication of the archives by Franca to the Library. The second element was a concert later at the Kennedy Center." Franca had invited President Bill Clinton and his wife, Hillary, to the opening ceremony, but at the last minute, a crisis in Africa stopped the president from participating. He sent the U.S. Marine band and color guard to represent him. In Madison Hall, where the opening ceremony took place, the color guard, in full regalia with rifles and five flags, presented arms for the national anthem, followed by a performance by the Marine band. It was a statesman's honor and the first time the Marine band and color guard had come to the Library of Congress. Franca donated Mulligan's baritone saxophone, which is in the showcase in the Gerry Mulligan Collection at the LOC.

During the band's rehearsal in the afternoon, Brookmeyer told Robinson, "They want you to play Mulligan's horn." "I knew he had a nice old Conn, similar to mine," Robinson said. "I had played with him one time, in 1989 or '90, when he did a guest spot with the Lionel Hampton Band, and I was in Hampton's band playing tenor. That kind of thing makes you a little bit nervous, but I said I'd take a crack at it.

"So, we had this rehearsal, and they brought out this big anvil flight case, and there's this beautiful Conn in there. I got it out and put my mouthpiece on and said, 'Hey, you know, it plays pretty great. It plays pretty much like mine.' So we rehearsed and then we packed the horn back in this heavy case. They said, 'Don't worry. You don't have to carry it. We're going to take it over to the venue for you.'

"Then it's time for the first ceremony. I come in, and there are all these dignitaries, Marine band and all this kind of stuff. I walk in, and Mulligan's horn is already set up on this podium on the stage, on this raised platform with all the lights shining on it. And it's got Mulligan's mouthpiece that was in the case. So I go and find somebody and I say, 'Where's the case? I need my mouthpiece, which is in the case.' And they say, 'Oh, they took the case back to the other building.' And there was no time to go get it. They said, 'Well, you'll just have to play with whatever's in there now.' I said, 'I can't do that. I don't know that mouthpiece. Is there a reed on it?' From a distance, it looked like there was.

"So, they start the whole thing. The Marine band marches in, and all this stuff is going on. And they have all these speeches. I'm sitting there just sweating. I'm thinking, 'What am I going to do? I don't know if I can even get a sound out of this thing.' Before I went on, they brought up this envoy from the Dalai Lama. He got up and said something spiritual in nature. They have these woven scarves. It's like a blessing if they put this scarf around your neck. I think he put the scarf around Franca. And then he put the scarf around the horn. And then they told me to come up. So I walked up there. And he said some blessing to me and put the scarf around my neck."

The Venerable Thamthog Rinpoche, abbot of the Namgyal Tantric Monastery of H. H. the Dalai Lama in Dharamsala, India, and spiritual director of the Center of Tibetan Studies in Milan, was a longtime friend of Gerry and Franca. He traveled from Italy for the dedication and draped a *khata*—a ceremonial scarf—on the saxophone and said: "Music is important to our lives and can have a positive or negative effect, depending on our motivation and the action of our mind. Gerry wrote beautiful music, very pure, which is a lasting and precious gift to the people of the world."

"I wasn't supposed to say anything," Robinson said. "I was just supposed to pick up the horn and play something. Instead, I picked up the microphone and said, 'I want to thank you very much for that blessing. And I'm sure I'm going to need it because I'm going to have to play this horn with Gerry Mulligan's mouthpiece and his twenty-five-year-old reed.' So, everybody laughed at that. I picked the thing up, and it had a hole in it. I didn't have a chance to warm up, test it, or anything. I decided to play 'Entente,' a Mulligan composition that I really love. I picked up the horn. I said, 'Here goes.' I blew into it, and it was absolutely glorious. The sound was fantastic. This old, dry, broken reed on this completely unfamiliar mouthpiece, and it just played fine. I was astonished. Then, later, we did the concert at Kennedy Center, and I had my mouthpiece back."

Mulligan said he was always conscious that the baritone saxophone was an octave lower than people are used to listening to. "They are much more attuned to a trumpet or an alto or even a soprano," he said. "The lower you go, the more effort it takes for an audience to concentrate."

Gary Giddins, in *Visions of Jazz: The First Century*, said that Mulligan is so recognized as a baritone saxophonist because he "is the only musician in history to win a popular following on that instrument, the only one to successfully extend the timbre of Harry Carney and develop an improvisational style in the horn's upper range. He initially studied piano, clarinet, and tenor, but the baritone best expressed his warmth, humor, and unerring ear for sensuous fabrics of sounds. Yet, he insisted he was less interested in playing solos than ensemble music—even in the context of his quartet. He was, as he proved from the beginning of his career, a master of blending instruments."

Jazz Journal International's Ian Kendall pointed out that "Mulligan certainly brought a mobility and lightness to the baritone that few other players have matched." Gordon Jack, in *Fifties Jazz Talk*, added: "In Gerry Mulligan's hands, the baritone saxophone, once considered an unwieldy section horn, became a vehicle for the most elegant and gracefully lyrical solo statements."

Jon Newsom, retired chief of the Music Division at the Library of Congress, believes Mulligan's sound as a saxophonist "was phenomenal. He could be compared with any classical virtuoso. I think he got better and better. He had enormous wind power. He used a number 5 reed, which is the stiffest reed there is. He remained a very strong and beautiful player right up to the end of his life."

17

'ACCEPTANCE OF JAZZ AS A SERIOUS MUSIC'

Jon Newsom began his career at the Library of Congress in 1966 as a music reference librarian. In the early 1990s, as assistant chief of the Music Division, he was interested in adding more jazz collections and decided to ask Gunther Schuller for advice. "I asked Gunther, 'Who would you go for? Who are the big musicians whose papers would be valuable to have?' The first one he mentioned was Gerry Mulligan." Schuller, as noted earlier, played French horn on the *Birth of the Cool* recording. "He also mentioned Charles Mingus, but Gerry was on the top of Gunther's list. So I did a very pro forma thing. I wrote Gerry a letter." Newsom did not receive an answer to his letter, but a couple of years later, he connected with Mulligan through a mutual friend.

Both Newsom and Mulligan were friends with David Raksin, a composer famous for writing the theme song to the 1944 film noir *Laura*. According to Newsom, "Gerry apparently called David and asked, 'What am I going to do with my papers?' David's papers were already coming to the Library of Congress, and he said, 'Well, just call Jon Newsom.' So Gerry did, and I took the train to Connecticut and spent a very pleasant day with him. The details were just purely the legal questions."

Upon entering the foyer outside the Performing Arts Reading Room of the Library of Congress, visitors are greeted by the Gerry Mulligan Collection, an impressive display that includes Mulligan's gold-plated Conn saxophone; several photographs, including one of him at the Grammy Awards at the moment he learned that *Walk on the Water* had won, and another of him at the receiving line at the 1995 Kennedy Center Honors ceremony, where he had been on the Artists Committee; music manuscripts in Mulligan's own hand; and album covers. On the back wall are woodblock print portraits of Mulligan in different shades by Antonio Frasconi.

There are more than five hundred special collections in the LOC's Music Division, but only one, the Mulligan collection, occupies this prominent space. "I was eager to do something rather special," Newsom explained to me, "not just because it was Gerry, but [because] the Music Division was known for its collections of classical composers and all of that. I thought we needed a more visible commitment to jazz. The idea was to have his saxophone. Libraries don't normally collect musical instruments, but the Library of Congress has one of the great instrument collections in the world. It has more than sixteen hundred flutes documenting the history of the flute, from the earliest times—from recorders to the most recent of the 20th century. We also have five Stradivarius instruments, and we have a number of very distinguished string instruments. So, we were not afraid of the idea of having Gerry's saxophone. I wanted to make a very visible commitment to jazz because we were hoping to attract more jazz performers and composers. I thought, 'Well, if we have Gerry's saxophone and can put it out someplace where people can see it, that would be a great plus.'

"I also had hopes and plans, which were partially realized, for making the instrument available to students. The instrument we got," he pointed out, "was the one he preferred to use in public performance. That's how we ended up with an exhibit for Gerry, because that was the way to show the world that the Library was committed to jazz. And to be honest, we were in a competitive situation with the Smithsonian. The Library of Congress is not a museum. We don't get tourists and that sort of stuff. The librarian under whom I worked during my last years, James Billington, was very keen on having a presence for the Library that would be more robust. I was a happy, dutiful employee, trying to make something as fancy and as useful as the Smithsonian.

"One thing we did," he continued, "with Gerry's saxophone, was to take it to the Interlochen Center for the Arts in Michigan, for a show where there was an opportunity for at least one student there to play Gerry's sax.

"With a saxophone, you don't have the insurance problems you had when you wanted to send Fritz Kreisler's violin to Indianapolis because it was valuated at $9 million. But Gerry's saxophone is a distinguished instrument, and it is an honor for a saxophonist who could play it. I don't think we would require them to use the number 5 reeds that Gerry used, but it was a good educational outreach. So, that's the story behind the saxophone and why the exhibit."

The Library of Congress's Music Division was formally created in 1896, and Newsom acknowledged that it has always been "identified with classical music. In 1938, when we first started broadcasting concerts in the Library, most Americans had never heard of chamber music. They knew about orchestras, and they knew about opera, but the idea of a chamber music series was revolutionary. And I think people began to hear the Budapest Quartet concerts broadcast across the country, and many people thought of the Library of Congress as nothing more than a place where the Budapest Quartet performed publicly on a weekly basis.

"With such a strong classical thrust," he continued," it took a long time for the people who were running things to accept jazz as something that was equally important. For example, in the late 1920s, the Library began to collect sound recordings, and we were offered the complete catalog of RCA Records. If we would have accepted that, we would have an unsurpassed collection from the RCA archives. But we said, 'Oh, just send us the classical stuff. We're not interested in jazz or popular music.' That was a mistake that we've had to spend many millions of dollars to correct by donations and also by purchases.

"So, with jazz, it took a while, and when I came to the Library in 1966, the man who hired me, Harold Spivacke, was the great chief who had held the hands of Mrs. Coolidge and Mrs. Whittall and took their money and made sure they were happy with the way it was spent."

Elizabeth Sprague Coolidge, who died three years before Newsom joined the LOC, expanded the vision and mission of the Library of Congress in 1924 by underwriting concerts, commissioning new music, and encouraging musicological scholarship. Gertrude Clarke Whittall, who died in 1965, donated the five Stradivari instruments to the Library in the mid-1930s, and in February 1936, the Gertrude Clarke Whittall Foundation was established at the Library to maintain the Stradivari instruments and to support their use in concerts. For many years, guest string quartets performed on the instruments in concerts until the Library decided to have a resident ensemble. The Budapest String Quartet was the resident ensemble from 1940 to 1962, followed by the Juilliard String Quartet.

"So jazz," Newsom said, "was definitely not even under consideration. Gradually, it happened, with pressure from me as I moved up in the ranks. When I finally got to be somebody in the hierarchy in the Music Division, I was given a free hand in going after some of these jazz collections." Newsom was promoted to head of the Reference Section in 1974. In 1978, he was named assistant chief of the Music Division and was named chief in 1997.

The acceptance of jazz as serious music, Newsom acknowledged, has "always been a battle. The whole ethos of music in the Library of Congress was shaped by these two great and powerful women—Mrs. Coolidge and Mrs. Whittall. Mrs. Coolidge gave us the auditorium and commissioned composers like Bartók and Schoenberg and Copeland and so many others. Mrs. Whittall gave us the five Strads [Stradivari] and money to support a resident string quartet."

Newsom said he grew up with *Birth of the Cool*. "While I'm not prepared to give a dissertation on all the threads of influence that recording had, you would find that it's very broad indeed. I see Gerry's influence as a young artist being probably the greatest. As he got older, I think he became an incredibly fine performer."

Earlier in this book, Newsom joined several others in expressing the belief that Mulligan deserved credit more than anyone else for the legacy of the *Birth of the Cool* recording. He believes another "enormous accomplishment" of Mulligan was "his ability to improvise in counterpoint with other musicians such as Chet Baker and Paul Desmond. He had so many albums with other great players. It's hard to think of other jazz musicians who had ability to that degree. He had that kind of ear. I was in his studio, and he once told me, 'I've never felt comfortable in front of a piece of music paper, just standing up and playing.' He was always arranging and composing in his head. And he could do that on his feet, thinking as a playing musician while he was performing either his arrangements or other people's stuff. He had an incredible contrapuntal ear that came absolutely natural to him. It's not a skill to exercise on paper; it's a skill he exercised playing live. It would be fun to get him together with J. S. Bach, who was also a pretty good improviser, to see what they might come up with.

"Gerry," Newsom continued, "was a linear thinker. He thought in lines, not chords. He's famous for the wonderful blending of lines. He once said to me, with reference to a jazz orchestra, 'You know, they're beginning to sound like a real good band because they are blending now.' He had a tremendous ear for that blend. Maurice Ravel, who was a great teacher of orchestrations, used to tell the students, 'Don't get so focused on chords. Think in terms of lines.' That is the key to good orchestration. You can see that in John Philip Sousa, another great orchestrator. Gerry thought in the lines; he thought melodically. That's probably why he was such a genius, not just as a soloist, but as a dualist or as a contrapuntalist. In some ways, I think Gerry will be remembered more as a collaborator than as a soloist. He played beautifully, but I think what is so unique about him is that he had this ability—and it's kind of a leadership thing—you get together with two or three people, it's like what makes a string quartet work or not work at all. You have to have great ears. You have to be able to hear, understand the other people, and you have to be able to do something that will hold them together.

"Some conductors have that. [Wilhelm] Furtwängler had it. There's a story about a rehearsal that was being led by the guy who prepared Furtwängler's orchestra. The timpanist didn't have much to do, so he would follow the whole proceedings with his miniature score. He was buried in this miniature score, listening to all that was going on, and, suddenly, the orchestra just pulled together and sounded so different. He looked up, and Furtwängler had just walked in. You have to believe in extrasensory perception or something for that kind of thing to happen.

"In jazz, [drummer] Louis Bellson had the same thing. He could sit in with a high school band, it would immediately click in ways that you could not explain in any technical process. Toscanini had it, too. That's a great gift, and Gerry had that. He's unique, and he doesn't fall neatly into one category. So I don't think he's gotten the recognition he deserves. He's one of the musicians whose complete works should be available as a matter of national preservation policy at all times."

The main thrust of the Library of Congress collection is to get people to play Mulligan's music, and Mulligan, according to LOC senior acquisitions specialist Loras Schissel, "was very pro that. He didn't want it just to be museum objects." Mulligan, added senior music reference specialist

Larry Appelbaum, "knew who he was. He understood his work, his accomplishments. For those of us who loved this music, you can see that this is a man who starts out as basically a writer. Those early arrangements for Elliot Lawrence, Gene Krupa, Claude Thornhill—they show a real creative imagination in the way he would voice certain things, his textures. It was different from the prevailing style of the day. And it always seemed to have this vision that became refined over the years. He had a unique voice. He had his own voice. That's really important in all the arts, but especially in jazz."

Appelbaum emphasized that access to the Mulligan Collection is considered very important to the Library. "It's enough that the music is in a safe place," he explained. "For most archives, that's enough. Just put it in a box and put the box on a shelf. But one of the great things about collections that are here is that we have the resources to accession, to process, to catalog, so that the collection is now organized, and there's a finding aid online, and that's how the world knows it's here. That way, people know what to request when they write to us. So that's the access side of preservation. That's why it's important that an institution not just acquire things but treat them responsibly by making them accessible to scholars and musicians and fans and researchers. There's a lot of music that many musicians and scholars would like to see, but they don't know where it is. They don't know how to find it. There's no central database of where all the music is."

The Mulligan Collection includes Mulligan's gold-plated baritone saxophone, photographs, music manuscripts, musical scores, record album covers, and information documenting his career, which lasted nearly fifty years. There are original manuscripts by other artists with whom Mulligan collaborated, such as Charlie Parker, Miles Davis, and Judy Holliday. The collection includes excerpts from Gerry Mulligan's oral autobiography, recorded in interviews with Ken Poston, director of the Los Angeles Jazz Institute. Material from the oral autobiography, as noted, has been quoted liberally in this book. The content for the LOC collection was edited by Newsom and his wife, Iris. "We both worked on it," Newsom said, "but Iris is a first-rate editor. She did a superb job."

At the reception on April 6, 1999, Dr. James Billington, Librarian of Congress, told the audience that "Gerry Mulligan, whose career spanned five decades, worked gracefully in many styles and with many artists, defying the categories that so often narrow our vision of a creative spirit. Gerry Mulligan would not—could not—be categorized, and he flourished through changing times, in many cultures, and with many musical voices, ranging from the baritone saxophone that was his principal instrument to the full orchestra."

Dr. Billington also described Franca Mulligan as "a valued friend with whom we have worked and will continue to work on many projects that have been inspired by Gerry's life and work."

Other jazz collections at the LOC include those of those of Charles Mingus, Ella Fitzgerald, Louis Bellson, Buddy Collette, and Gerald Wilson. There is also a collection of photographs of jazz artists by William Gottlieb.

18

'EVERYBODY'S A FILM CRITIC'

In addition to *I Want to Live!*, *The Subterraneans*, and *The Bells Are Ringing*, Gerry Mulligan was involved in several other film projects. In the '60s, he was asked to write the soundtrack for the 1967 movie *Luv*, directed by Clive Donner and based on the Broadway play of the same name written by Murray Schisgal. The movie starred Jack Lemmon, Peter Falk, and Elaine May.

The film was not a success, and Mulligan was unhappy with the soundtrack. "On Broadway," he said, "it was a two-character comedy that all took place on one set. The comedic acting in the movie was terrific, but the three styles [of Lemmon, Falk, and May] were three totally different styles of comedy. I had this idea of approaching it with a Dixieland, loose-jointed kind of thing. [Donner] said, 'Terrific,' but we got away from the original idea. For years, I would wake up in the middle of the night thinking about this project and what I wanted to do. I would do anything if I could do that score over again."

In his book *Lemmon,* Don Widener described *Luv* as "one of those Hollywood oddities—the picture that gets produced despite the fact that everyone agrees it is certain to bomb—it did."

In 1977, Mulligan received another opportunity to score a feature film, when he was contacted by Denise Petitdidier, the producer of a French film called *La Menace,* to be directed by Alain Corneau. It was a thriller starting Yves Montand. "I was able to put into practice some of the things I'd learned not to do in the *Luv* score," Mulligan explained. "They had sent me an English translation of a shortened version of the script. Then, Alain Corneau came to talk to me to flesh out the outline he had made. He talked the movie through. Then he invited me to come to France to go to the place they had picked out for the location. So Franca and I took off for Bordeaux."

Franca recalled that while Mulligan was meeting with Corneau, "Gerry was taking notes, but they were not written notes, they were musical notes. He had already written the whole score on the spot. Alain Corneau said, 'I knew you were a genius, but that's incredible.' He had only a month to present the recording, to find the musicians, to write the music."

During this time, composer/arranger/pianist Dave Grusin was visiting the Mulligans in Connecticut and offered to help Mulligan organize the tracks and help finish the project. Grusin also played keyboards for a recording session that took place at Don Elliott's studio in Westport, Connecticut. The other musicians on the recording were: Tom Fay and Derek Smith, piano; Jay Leonhart and Jack Six, bass; Michael Di Pasqua and Bobby Rosengarden, drums; and Peter Levin and Edward Walsh, synthesizer.

"We arrived in Paris with the completed soundtrack," Franca recalled, "which Alain quickly set to be played along with the film—that Gerry and I were seeing for the first time. The music matched to the split second; they couldn't believe it." Mulligan recalled, "Alain and I were ecstatic because all of my things worked—not only the timings, but the mood worked for what was going on on the screen."

But: "When they started playing it for U.S. and Canadian distributors," Mulligan said, "they suggested cuts—everybody's a film critic. Well, they made a mishmash of it."

Raymond Horricks, writing in the February 3, 1998, issue of *Crescendo & Jazz Music*, considered the music of *La Menace* "easily the most satisfying film work of [Mulligan's] career . . . for *La Menace*, he was totally master of the music . . . Mulligan the composer is suitably dutiful towards director Alain Corneau's story line, changes of mood and atmosphere . . . in the actual music-making, Gerry's is the only horn. He uses three pianists—acoustic and electric—including Dave Grusin, with whom he was getting into a friendly and lasting association; plus Moog and Oberheim synthesizers. He stays mainly on baritone, with some overdubbed soprano sax, and, for 'The Pantomimist,' a favored 'woody' clarinet; reminding one of how much Gerry admired Danny Polo and Irving Fazola within Claude Thornhill's Orchestra." Grusin and Mulligan had played together since the 1950s and, according to Franca, "had a longtime friendship and lasting association."

Since some of the songs were cut from the U.S. and Canadian versions of the soundtrack, Mulligan wanted to release an album that would include everything he composed for the movie. The resulting album, *Watching & Waiting*, was released by DRG in 1982 and reissued in 1999.

Jazz writer and producer Doug Payne, reviewing the 1999 reissue on his blog, pointed out that "The French arm of CBS issued a soundtrack to *La Menace* in 1977. Since the film, known in English-speaking climes as *The Threat*, never had a proper American release, the music had also never had a proper American release until this CD release." Payne described Mulligan, on the soundtrack, as "less an improviser and more a mood setter. But the wonderful clarification he brings to his horn parts sings with the overall goal of the piece. Like any composer, he isn't aiming to be the star soloist. He is suggesting the right setting for the film he is accompanying. But his beautifully signature-sounding baritone is bountiful on such pieces as 'Introspect,' 'Watching and Waiting,' and the lovely 'Vines of Bordeaux.' *La Menace/Watching & Waiting* makes for some wonderful listening . . ."

Several other film credits throughout Mulligan's career included:

- A miniscule acting role as a bandleader in *The Rat Race* with Tony Curtis and Debbie Reynolds. (He also dubbed Curtis's sax playing.)
- Composition of the title song for the movie *A Thousand Clowns*, with Jason Robards and Barbara Harris (1965). This was Mulligan's first screen composer's credit.
- Performance on the André Previn soundtrack of *The Fortune Cookie* with Jack Lemmon and Walter Matthau (1966)
- Featured performance on Quincy Jones's soundtrack for *The Hot Rock*, starring Robert Redford (1972)
- Playing of soprano and baritone saxophone on Sergio Mendes's soundtrack for the documentary *Pele* (1977)

In 1997, the year after his death, Mulligan's compositions and/or performances appeared in three films: *I'm Not Rappaport* (for which he composed and performed the theme, which was heard throughout the movie); *L.A. Confidential* (which featured "Makin' Whoopee," performed by Mulligan and Chet Baker); and *The Ice Storm* (which featured "Night Lights," composed and performed by Mulligan from an album of the same name). According to Franca, the playwright Herb Gardner had called to remind Mulligan that the musician had agreed to write the score for the movie version of *I'm Not Rappaport.* Franca recalled: "Gerry said, 'I'm going to play it to you on my soprano; if you wish, record it.' Gerry played it over the phone, and Herb recorded it. Luckily, it was a good-quality recording, since Gerry passed away in January 1996. Herb was left with the phone recording, which he used as the soundtrack for the film."

David Amram believes that, had he chosen to, "Gerry could have been a great actor. In *The Subterraneans*, he played a priest, and he was terrific. He just had a natural charisma and charm and grace and a great wit."

19

'ONE OF THE MOST BRILLIANT PERFORMANCES EVER'

"Gerry Mulligan limped on stage in a stiff-legged gait, made a few wry comments to the crowd, then lifted his big baritone saxophone to his lips and played. He was gaunt in frame but still bright of eye. And he made his horn sing in a tone so warm and smooth it was almost a purr. It was last October 29, and Mulligan was the featured performer on the final night of the Hollywood Jazz Festival. No one said so, but he was a dying man."

Matt Schudel, a jazz columnist for the *Sun-Sentinel* of Broward and South Palm Beach, Florida, wrote those words on February 4, 1996, a little more than two weeks after Gerry Mulligan died on January 20.

"For months," Schudel continued, "there had been rumors that Mulligan had liver cancer, and he had confided as much to his friends. He kept his pain hidden, though, choosing to give his final breath to the music. Out of sight of the audience, he was brought to the edge of the stage in a wheelchair, then walked haltingly, but unaided, into the spotlight and the applause. He looked frail, holding his 16-pound saxophone, but he sounded great, with the same haunting, pearl-like tone he had discovered in the 1940s."

Mulligan had been included on the Artists Committee for the 1995

Kennedy Center Honors for the Performing Arts, and he and Franca attended the Kennedy Center ceremonies in December 1995. A photo of them in the receiving line to greet the Clintons at the White House clearly reveals that he was in failing health.

In November 1995, Mulligan played aboard a Caribbean jazz cruise on the S.S. *Norway*. Several of his closest friends—including Johnny Mandel, Phil Woods, and jazz critic and historian Gene Lees—were on the cruise. Lees, in *Arranging the Score: Portraits of the Great Arrangers*, wrote that he "had been hearing rumors for months that Gerry's health was failing rapidly. Bobby Rosengarden, his neighbor in Connecticut, told me that Gerry was undergoing chemotherapy in Boston. Gerry would tell me that it was for treatment of a liver condition consequent of a case of hepatitis years ago. He said he only felt bad after the treatment. I know of only one thing that chemotherapy is used for.

"Phil Woods was on the cruise, performing in the same week as Gerry's group . . . Johnny Mandel came along as a passenger, just to hang with his friends, and the week developed into that, a hangout of Johnny, Phil, Gerry, and me. But Gerry was very weak. His red-blond hair long ago had turned paper white. But his skin now had a transparent look; the bluish veins in his hands stood out. And he was in a wheelchair much of the time, using a cane the rest of it."

At Mulligan's performance, Lees recalled, "He hobbled onstage and sat on a stool. And the quartet began to play. It was one of the best groups Gerry ever led. And it was some of the finest and most inventive playing I ever heard from him in the thirty-six years of our friendship, not to mention the years long before we met, when his LPs were high on the list of my favorite records."

Woods described it to me as "one of the most brilliant performances ever. We all knew he was sick and wasn't going to be around too much longer. We were just awestruck at the depth of emotion that poured out of his baritone. He played 'Curtains,' that wonderful song of his and one of my favorites of his compositions. It was one of the greatest performances of any artist that I've ever heard." Everyone, according to Mandel, "was reduced to tears—not because it was so sad, but because it was so beautiful. Gerry had transcended even himself."

Lees thought "the rapport of the group was amazing, particularly Gerry's telepathic communication with the outstanding pianist Ted Rosenthal. I was in awe of what I heard . . . There was one piece that he played in which the interplay with Rosenthal left me with my jaw hanging down. So exquisite was the structure of what he, bassist Dean Johnson, and drummer Ron Vincent did, that, afterwards, I told him, 'Gerry, I am not sure that this should any longer be called jazz. It seems to be some kind of new end-of-the-century classical music." Franca, his wife, told me later he quoted that with great pleasure."

Rosenthal said the members of the quartet "really didn't know too many details about Gerry's health. We saw him, for one of the first times, using a wheelchair. But when you talked to him and played with him, he was pretty much his feisty self, a little mellower, perhaps, than when I first met him. We never dreamed that this could be one of our last gigs with him." Rosenthal said that a unique rapport had developed between himself and Mulligan. "By then," he said, "we had some history between us, and I guess he had a trust in what I was doing, so I could bust out now and then, and he would sort of nod approvingly. I guess a few people picked up on that we had some nice musical moments between us."

Mulligan had two more performances on the cruise, but Lees, Woods, and Mandel couldn't bear to attend. "Both of them," Lees wrote, "felt as I did; they couldn't endure a second performance. Such was the tearing of emotions in two directions—ecstasy at the level of Mulligan's music and agony at the frailty of his health."

The next day, Lees said, Mulligan asked the three of them to come by his room. "We went up to the top deck. Gerry was never enamored of the sun; with his blonde, now white eyelashes, its glare bothered him. But we went up, and I took a camera. Franca photographed the four of us."

Mulligan telephoned Lees on New Year's Eve. "He told me how much he loved a lyric I had written at his request for one of his tunes, 'I Hear the Shadows Dancing.' He said, 'It makes me cry.' But then he became cheerful and said he was feeling well and lectured me a little about taking care of my own health."

Lees had an "ominous feeling afterwards that it was a farewell call. Bill Holman, whom he called in mid-January, got the same feeling, and so did Mandel, whom he phoned around the 10th . . . His farewell to his friends was as graceful as his playing."

Harold Danko recalled the last time he saw Mulligan, when, as far as he knew, Mulligan was still in good health. "I had moved to New Haven, and he invited me over. I remember that I noticed Gerry had got mellower, almost sentimental. I thought, 'Wait a minute. I want to see the old Gerry.' It was touching that he just wanted to get together. He said, 'Do you want me to play a tune?' We played 'Walk on the Water.' I think that's the last time I played with him."

Mulligan's last album, *Dragonfly*, one of three on the Telarc label, was recorded in July 1995. John Scofield savored the memory of playing on that album. "He brought me in as a guest," he recalled. "I remember [coproducer] John Snyder had told me, 'Listen, Gerry's sick.' I guess he was battling cancer at the time. I thought he played great on that date." Warren Vaché, who played cornet on the recording, had never performed or recorded with Mulligan before and appreciated the opportunity to be part of *Dragonfly*. "My time with him was brief and pleasant," Vaché said. "He was a very creative guy. His attention to detail was remarkable."

All ten selections on the album were Mulligan original compositions. In the liner notes, he broke the album down like a dramatic performance. "THE PLOT," he wrote, was to: "Take a batch of brand new tunes . . . At this point the tunes are in various stages of completion, and it's time for players' input—keys, tempos, grooves, etc."

Next were, "THE PLAYERS—Call up several good friends, old and new, who just happen to be among the greatest jazz musicians in the world and send them copies of the tunes.

"When Dave Grusin plays my tunes, I always learn something new, so for me, it's a luxury to have him on this (or any other) album! The fact that both Dave and [saxophonist] Grover Washington were only available on the same day out of the whole year was so obviously a good omen that I felt as if the album was already half finished!

"John Scofield and Dave Samuels played with me in a sextet in the '70s. Some of their solo interplay on this recording . . . is exquisite, and, with the addition of Warren Vaché to this group I fulfilled a dream I've had since the '70s. Warren, in my opinion, is the best cornet player anywhere. When Ted Rosenthal joins in, it's as if four people are negotiating the same tightrope." The trumpeter Ryan Kisor was included, Mulligan explained, because Mulligan had heard him play at a Lincoln Center tribute to Art

Farmer. "Ryan was very enthusiastic and came in loaded for bear and with obvious great respect for Art and Art's playing."

Finally: "THE PERFORMANCE—I could see from the way the schedule was evolving, I would need help to have the actual transposed and copied parts ready when we needed them. [Trumpeter] Mike Mossman and [trombonist] Slide Hampton were my angels in disguise. I knew I'd be on tour in Europe with my quartet, along with Dave Brubeck's quartet, and there would be little writing time on the road . . . By the time we got back to New York, everything was ready to go for the last series of dates. Slide has his orchestrations all done, and I still had enough time to finish up my charts."

As for his quartet, "I've never been one to get much writing done while traveling, but on this trip, we were having entirely too much fun . . . Dean, Ron, and Ted have been with me as the other three-fourths of the Gerry Mulligan Quartet for years and years. In fact, we had a dinner party in Oslo, Norway, to celebrate Dean's tenth anniversary! A big coincidence is that we were playing the same hall as on Dean's first night ten years ago . . . Franca is my indispensable third ear, all the way through, as always."

The *Chicago Tribune*'s Howard Reich, writing in the January 28, 1996 issue, felt *Dragonfly* confirmed that "Mulligan remained a soft-spoken iconoclast to the end . . . The shimmering textures, intricate counterpoint, and nocturnal feeling of *Dragonfly* neatly sums up his idiom."

Raymond Horricks, in the August 9, 1997 issue of *Crescendo & Jazz Music*, said *Dragonfly* reaffirmed "Gerry's melodic, harmonic and inspirational powers . . . His own sax improvisations flow with brilliance throughout. Whether or not the collection was put together with a premonition of coming illness, I don't know. But it was certainly put together with love and majesty . . ."

Another album, *Midas Touch*, recorded live by Mulligan in May 1995, was released by Concord in 2003. It also demonstrates the brilliance and intensity of his playing—even as his health was failing—and the camaraderie of the Rosenthal-Johnson-Vincent rhythm section. "This previously unreleased collection of seven Mulligan tunes," wrote David Franklin, in the June 2003 issue of *Jazz Times,* "performed by a superb, well-rehearsed quartet (plus a duet with Dave Brubeck on the standard 'These Foolish Things'), shows the saxophonist at his most sensitive, as on the moving

'Wallflower' and at his most visceral, as on the high-flying 'Sun on the Stairs' and the obligatory 'Walkin' Shoes.' Mulligan's smooth distinctive tone, his lyrical expressiveness, his joyous swing, and his composer's ability to create logical, coherently constructed choruses are all fully on display. And the excellence of his rhythm section—pianist Ted Rosenthal, bassist Dean Johnson, and drummer Ron Vincent—helped assure a top-notch product, Rosenthal's prodigious technique and imaginative improvisations being particularly noteworthy. The final duet with Brubeck, which starts out as a ballad before the pianist switches to a sprightly double-time stride accompaniment, is a charming bonus."

Franca told me that when Mulligan found out "he was not having a long time to live, he said, 'Franca, I don't get angry anymore. Where has my anger gone?' He explained to me that, when he was depressed, anger was the best remedy to get out of the depression because of the adrenaline. He was using the anger to get out of being down—not being able to write or if he didn't have enough work.

"But I saw him when they told him he didn't have much longer to live. At that point, instead of getting angry, he used it to reflect on the quality of life. He started thinking even more about others. The night that they told him he had probably one day to live, we were in the hospital, and, for the first time, I started crying, and he opened his arms, and he was trying to console me. He said, 'Franca, don't forget to send the money' to a musician who needed it for his cancer operation. That's what was Gerry."

Elliot Lawrence received a phone call in the middle of the night. "It was Gerry," he said. "He wanted to talk to me. What he wanted to tell me is, 'Elliot, the best time I ever had in my life was when we were seventeen years old together, and we started out in writing.' This broke me up. It was my last contact with Gerry."

Lees received a call from Franca on the morning of January 20. "I said, 'How are you?' She said, 'I'm fine.' I said, 'How's Gerry?' And she said, 'Gerry's dead.' It was like a body blow, although I could recall all the auguries of the past months."

Riccardo Muti, in the *Listen: Gerry Mulligan* video, talked about the void that Mulligan's death had created. "I will not be able to turn and see his white hair surrounding his inspired face. This is a great loss for me personally and also for the musicians of the theater."

There were many tributes and remembrances, of course. In the June 1996 issue of *Jazz Times*, Ira Gitler recalled a trip to Japan with Mulligan. "Gerry," he said, "was witty in an acerbic way. In 1982, we were with him at a jazz festival in Madarao, Japan. My wife and I and jazz film maven David Chertok and his wife were standing to the side of the stage listening to a big band of Japanese teenage boys and girls, who clad in white, all starched and clean, were playing Glenn Miller charts from memory. The shuttle bus from the hotel deposited Mulligan nearby—I think his orchestra was playing a set later in the afternoon—and, as he approached us, Corinne Chertok said to him, with a nod toward the stage, 'Aren't they cute?' As he turned to walk away, without missing a beat, Gerry snapped, 'Jazz and cute don't mix.'

"Jazz and Gerry did. He never compromised his high ideals—a true artist. Gerry Mulligan gave us a lot of music, but he should have lived longer. He had so much more to say."

Howard Lucraft first met Mulligan at the Haig on the opening night of the pianoless quartet. An interview he conducted a few days later with a "nervous" Mulligan was, by Lucraft's admission "not remarkable." What was remarkable, Lucraft wrote in the February-March 1996 issue of *Crescendo & Jazz Music*, was the memory of "that commanding, hirsute figure, latterly with snowy hair and beard but, earlier, with a shock of flaming red hair, swaying with that large horn and swinging vigorously with those incisive, logical, and melodical phrases."

In April 1996, *Down Beat*'s John McDonough reminisced about Mulligan's compulsiveness when it came to spontaneously sitting in. "My most vivid recollection of Mulligan," he wrote, "goes back to a memorable White House jazz concert in 1978. Jazz was still young enough that its entire history could be gathered on one stage. Musicians from Eubie Blake to Cecil Taylor were there. Some played and some were asked to make introductions. Among the latter was Mulligan, who left his bari in Connecticut. But, as dusk settled over the South Lawn, Lionel Hampton started calling everyone up on stage for the final jam session. Mulligan suddenly seemed to grow mad with frustration at the thought of sitting this one out. Without his baritone and desperate, he cast about for a horn, any horn. Finally he managed to persuade the clarinetist of a New Orleans brass band to loan him his instrument, then bounded up on stage just in time to join in 'Flying Home' and 'In the Good Old Summertime.'"

Stories about Mulligan's inability to turn down an opportunity to perform, even when he wasn't planning to play, are legendary among his band members and friends.

Keith O'Quinn, a trombonist in the Concert Jazz Band of the late '70s and early '80s, invited Mulligan to his wedding in 1980. "For our wedding," O'Quinn told me, "we wanted to have really good music. And we decided we really wanted to have a jazz group rather than just something for dancing, since most of the guests were musicians or somehow related to the music business. My wife Pam's father is Joe Shepley, a great New York trumpet player, and he suggested that we see if Al Cohn would be into doing the party with a rhythm section. I really didn't think he'd do it, but Joe was a friend of Al's, and when Joe called him, he accepted the gig. The band was to be Al, John Bunch on piano, John Beal on bass, and a local Westchester drummer, Peter Scatt.

"I had sent an invitation to Gerry and Franca, hoping they would come, and I got a reply that they might make it but weren't sure. We were getting married at a church in Mount Vernon, New York, and the reception was at a beautiful restaurant in Tarrytown. After the wedding ceremony, we were greeting guests and coming out of the church, and I was surprised to suddenly see Gerry and Franca. As Gerry congratulated us, he handed me a wrapped gift and said he was really sorry, but he had a bunch of work to catch up on and wouldn't be able to come to the reception. I told him how sorry I was that he wasn't coming, but that I understood. Then I told him that the party should be a lot of fun, and the music would be great because Al Cohn was playing the reception. His jaw sort of dropped. Gerry *loved* Al Cohn and really admired him as a musician. He had written some of the greatest arrangements for Gerry's big band. He suddenly said, 'Well, let me see what I can do. I have to run home.' He lived in Darien, Connecticut, which was about forty minutes away. About an hour into the reception, he showed up. He had gone home and gotten his horn, and he sat in with Al for several tunes. It was a real honor and pleasure for all of us to hear both of those guys. Gerry always loved to play, and we were really fortunate that we had Al to help lure him there."

David Amram remembered having a gig in Stamford, Connecticut, with saxophonist Jerry Dodgion. "Gerry said, 'Man, I'm going to come with Franca.' I said, 'Franca, it's so nice of you and Gerry to come and just hang out, and you can have a night off together.' She said, 'Well, that hardly ever happens.' About the third tune, Gerry comes up and says, 'Man, can I play the piano?' I said, 'Sure,' so he sat and played fantastic. I said to Franca, 'I really apologize.' She said, 'No, no, I could see him sitting there, dying to play. I thought maybe he'd play one tune, and then I saw how much you guys all loved it.'" (In early 2015, Franca received an email from Amram crediting her with giving Mulligan "the best and most productive years of his life, as well as the healthiest and happiest he ever had . . . I appreciate and admire all that you have done to have his music available to be played by being able to download it. It is every composer's dream to have their music stay alive, and what you have done will insure his music always being there."

"Gerry," said Raymond Horricks, "never missed an opportunity to blow alongside anyone—of whatever jazz school—he believed could stimulate his own playing."

Of all the tributes that poured in, though, perhaps the most noteworthy was a letter Franca received from President Bill Clinton. "Dear Franca," he wrote, "Hillary and I were deeply saddened by Gerry's death, and our hearts go out to you at this difficult time.

"Gerry truly made a difference during his lifetime. He was a brilliant innovator in the world of jazz, advancing and expanding his craft and leaving a powerful legacy that musicians and jazz lovers will long admire and study. As you know, he was an inspiration to me from the time I was a young man—I will always treasure our visit together last month at the Kennedy Center Honors."

That was the typewritten portion of the letter, but below it, in Clinton's handwriting, was this additional note: *"No one ever played that horn like he did, and no one ever will . . ."*

20

'NOBODY REALLY PLAYED LIKE HIM'

Since Mulligan's death, there have been several live and recorded tributes to him, in addition to the Library of Congress event in April 1999, featuring Scott Robinson, and the 1998 three-baritone recording by Smulyan, Brignola, and Cuber.

On January 20, 1996, the day of Mulligan's death, a spontaneous tribute was presented in Chicago. At what was to be a Chicago all-stars jam session at the Bop Shop, tenor saxophonist Von Freeman announced to the audience, "This is for a great saxophone player who just left us—Gerry Mulligan." The *Chicago Tribune*'s Howard Reich, writing on January 22, 1996, said the evening then "unfolded as a musical homage from one reed titan to another. But there was more than mere sentiment coming from Freeman's tenor horn. As the solo progressed, the ornamentation became more intricate, the harmonies bolder, the rhythmic ideas more finely articulated. By the time Freeman brought the band back into the action, he already had said a great deal about his admiration of Mulligan's art."

Later in the evening, saxophonist Jeff Newell arrived and, according to Reich, "picked up where Freeman had left off. Newell's ethereal reading of 'I Remember You' clearly represented another Mulligan tribute. Certainly the airiness of Newell's tone here evoked the sound of Mulligan's horn."

On October 19, 1996, at New York's Lincoln Center, Wynton Marsalis and the Lincoln Center Jazz Orchestra performed a concert titled "Jeru: The Music of Gerry Mulligan." Guest soloists were Art Farmer on trumpet and Joe Temperley on baritone saxophone. The program encompassed music covering Mulligan's full career, with emphasis on the Concert Jazz Band and *The Age of Steam* album. President Bill Clinton wrote a special welcome, which was read to the audience by Marsalis prior to the performance. As a personal present to Mulligan, Marsalis had his New Orleans band come onstage. Before his death, Mulligan had told Franca, "I would like to have Wynton Marsalis and the New Orleans Band perform at my funeral." Since there was no funeral, this was the first opportunity Marsalis had to honor Mulligan's request. *Down Beat*'s Larry Birnbaum described the scene in the January 1997 issue: "Standing at the lip of the stage, Marsalis, joined by Herlin Riley on bass drum, Wayne Goodman on trombone, Wes Anderson on alto sax, and Crescent City guests Michael White on clarinet and Shannon Powell on snare drum, played the solemn 'Free as a Bird,' followed by the rollicking 'Didn't He Ramble.' It was hardly Mulligan's style, but he surely would have enjoyed it."

Producer Hank O'Neal organized a Mulligan tribute album: *The Gerry Mulligan Songbook* (January 1997, Chiaroscuro), a duo-piano album with Bill Charlap and Ted Rosenthal, bassist Dean Johnson, and drummer Ron Vincent. It contained eleven tracks of music either written by or associated with Mulligan such as "Line for Lyons," "Walkin' Shoes" and "Song for Strayhorn."

Playing Mulligan's music with Charlap, Rosenthal said, enabled them to "enjoy the little harmonic and voicing movements that were kind of intrinsic in Gerry's music, noticing what made those things really special. Even if they were done with a pianoless group, they could translate nicely to the piano. That was kind of a substantial aspect to his music because he played the piano himself, so that really made them transfer to the piano."

Rosenthal also played on a subsequent album called *Thank You, Gerry! Our Tribute to Gerry Mulligan* (Arcadia Jazz, June 1998). "Dean Johnson, Ron Vincent, and Ted Rosenthal," Franca said, "asked me if they could form a Gerry Mulligan all-star band, which included Bob Brookmeyer on trombone, Lee Konitz on alto saxophone, and Randy Brecker on trumpet."

The initial concert series was held at New York's Blue Note jazz club in April 1997. The tribute band returned to the Blue Note in 1998 and appeared in other concert halls and clubs. "We had a nice, short run for about two years," Rosenthal said.

Of all the tributes to Mulligan, AllMusic's Ken Dryden considers *Thank*

You, Gerry! "easily the best of the lot . . . There are a number of reasons why this session turned out so well: the eight Mulligan compositions don't just include the early hits, but also challenging works from late in his career; the interplay between the players and their individual solos are never less than superb; finally, they felt no need to include a baritone saxophonist on the date, as Brookmeyer's valve trombone consistently achieves the lyrical feeling that Mulligan would have added on his baritone sax if he had been present, even if the two instruments aren't that close in sound." According to Johnson, "We didn't use a baritone because nobody really played like him. You couldn't really make a new Mulligan."

In October 2000, Telarc Jazz released *The Art of Gerry Mulligan: The Final Recordings*, a compilation of his last three albums, all recorded on the label: *Paraiso, Dream a Little Dream*, and *Dragonfly*.

That recording, according to the All About Jazz staff, in a review published on December 1, 2000, "not only shows that Mulligan's unparalleled talent for accessible improvisation remained intact, even as his health declined, but also suggests that his wide range of creative interests remained unpredictable." On *Paraiso*, they pointed out, "Floating through songs like 'Wave' or 'North Atlantic Rim,' Mulligan plays liltingly in unison or in accompaniment with singer Jane Duboc, quite a feat considering the difficulty of playing his instrument in what is basically a tenor range . . . The tracks from *Dragonfly* pursue a bluesier and more bop-based style . . . And then *Dream a Little Dream* records Mulligan's last great group with Ted Rosenthal on piano, Dean Johnson on bass, and Ron Vincent on drums."

There were two separate tributes in Southern California five and six years after Mulligan's death. They were organized by Ken Poston, the concert producer and jazz historian who helped Mulligan record his oral autobiography (quoted liberally throughout this book). On April 1, 2001, a two-part concert was held at the Gerald R. Daniel Recital Hall in Long Beach. The first half was performed by the Cal State Studio One Jazz Ensemble conducted by Dr. Neal Finn. The second half consisted of a quartet—the rhythm section of Rosenthal, Johnson, and Vincent, with baritone saxophonist Bill Perkins. Cal State Ensemble was a student group, and the *Los Angeles Times*'s Don Heckman wrote on April 3, 2001 that the playing was "generally well crafted . . . providing an overview of Mulligan works ranging from his early Gene Krupa charts and his own late-'50s big-band arrangements to his writing for Stan Kenton and his Concert Jazz Band."

Heckman praised Perkins's "dark-timbred baritone sound, so similar to Mulligan's, despite an obvious lack of rehearsal time." But he saved his greatest praise for the rhythm section, which he described as "musically precise but ineffably swinging, soloing individually with imagination and skill, producing the familiar understated Mulliganesque drive . . . their playing was the program's clearest link—and the most appropriate tribute—to the multiplicity of elements that made up the Mulligan musical persona."

The second California tribute was presented by the Los Angeles Jazz Institute on July 26, 2002, at the Hermosa Playhouse. The program consisted of selections associated with the tentette, as well as music Mulligan composed for the Stan Kenton Orchestra upon his arrival in California in the early '50s. The best-known composition from the Kenton days is "Youngblood," and the interpretation played by the L.A. musicians, according to Heckman, in the August 2, 2001 issue of the *Times*, was "magnificent, a stunning example of Mulligan's unerring ability to retain his primal rhythmic drive and love for melody in everything he did." Fittingly, both the tentette and larger band were conducted by Bill Holman, whose arrangements had such an impact on the Concert Jazz Band.

In addition to his three-baritone saxophone album in 1998, Smulyan participated in a live tribute to Mulligan in 2012. The concert, on February 29, was presented by the Julliard Jazz Orchestra at Julliard's Peter Jay Sharp Theater with Smulyan as the guest artist. Called the "Gerry Mulligan Tribute Concert," it was held to introduce the Gerry & Franca Mulligan Scholarship, and, during the evening, one of Mulligan's baritone saxophones was donated to Juilliard. Juilliard student Jordan Pettay was the first recipient of the scholarship and performed with the JJO. The scholarship was established by the Gerry & Franca Mulligan Foundation to support young musicians and to perpetuate the music of Gerry Mulligan.

Smulyan remembers the event as "a beautiful night of music, just to hear those arrangements again—most of them from the Concert Jazz Band, some from Elliot Lawrence, some from *Birth of the Cool.*"

Wynton Marsalis and Jazz at Lincoln Center presented "The Music of

Gerry Mulligan & John Lewis" as part of a "Birth of the Cool Festival" on January 18 and 19, 2013. The Jazz at Lincoln Center Orchestra explored the full breadth of Mulligan's compositions, from "Walkin' Shoes" to "Lonesome Boulevard."

In October 1995, a few months prior to Mulligan's death, Franca and the Venerable Thamthog Rinpoche organized a benefit concert in Milan to raise money for the Sera Je Monastery, with Mulligan performing with the Buddhist monks, and with singer Ornella Vanoni, accompanied by a trio of two guitars and a bass, as a rhythm section. During the press conference prior to the concert, the journalists asked Mulligan how he came to be performing with the monks, and he responded that "Franca follows the Buddhist philosophy." They asked him if he was a Buddhist, and he responded, "I think in the back of my mind, always was."

In March 2014, there were two events in Liege, Belgium, celebrating not only Mulligan's music, but also his drawings, which were shown in public for the first time. The drawings, around one hundred seventy watercolors, were exhibited at the Académie Royale des Beaux Arts de Liège. There were two concerts at the Conservatoire Royal de Liège, one by a symphony orchestra and one by the Conservatory Octet's Quartet Band. The art exhibit included a book/catalog with all of Mulligan's drawings, some photos, and a handwritten note by Mulligan.

Franca spoke at both the art exhibit and at one of the concerts. "Gerry," she said, "is one of the great figures, not just in jazz, but also of the artistic life of the 20th century. He had a deep appreciation for history, literature, art, architecture, engineering, and nature." She also reminded her audiences that Mulligan was "a self-taught composer . . . He was a real artist in the universal sense of the word, and he was gifted with a special sensibility, a great sense of humor, and the capacity to express it, not only through his music, but also through his thoughts and in the way he lived his everyday life."

21

'MELODICISM SECOND TO NONE'

"I don't consider myself jazz, particularly. My favorite musicians were jazz musicians, but I didn't start out being one myself. Sometimes, it's presumptuous to call myself one. I'm a composer. I'm involved with my own music out of various influences. I suppose in the panoply of existing American music, there are more things in what is called 'jazz' that I prefer than in any other form."

—Gerry Mulligan, *Down Beat,* July 15, 1976

Gerry Mulligan was a composer, arranger, bandleader, musician. If he excelled at only one of those four disciplines, we would remember him. As he acknowledged, he would be mostly associated with jazz, but not completely. Jazz, some would say, is America's classical music, so what is Mulligan's legacy?

I began this book, in the introduction, with a quote from Jon Newsom, retired chief of the Music Division of the Library of Congress, expressed in the documentary *Listen: Gerry Mulligan.* "Gerry Mulligan," Newsom said, "is one of the truly unique figures in American music, not just speaking of jazz, but of music in a broader, general way." I believe that's so. He was as comfortable on Broadway as he was at Birdland, and, as has been documented earlier in this book, he was at home in a symphonic setting as well.

When I interviewed Mulligan in 1981, he indicated to me that his dream was to have a television show, patterned after Lawrence Welk's.

"For years," he told me, "I've been wanting to do a variety show based around a band. I would have guests—singers and comics—and present things in a grown-up way. Probably the most successful musical show on television was *The Lawrence Welk Show*. I don't see why a show like that can't be done based around another kind of music."

The *Los Angeles Times*'s Don Heckman wrote that Mulligan "appears to have been taken for granted by the jazz world." In his obituary of Mulligan, which appeared on January 25, 1996, Heckman speculated that "part of the problem, of course, was his versatility. Soloist, bandleader, composer, arranger, and songwriter, he touched all the important musical bases, inspiring other musicians from the beginning." And Mulligan's sound on baritone saxophone, Heckman added, was "immediately recognizable, a rich, warm inviting timbre. Smooth and flowing in ballads, overflowing with energy and vigor in up-tempos, it was a sound that spoke, always irresistibly, in the dialect of the urgent, propulsive swing that is at the heart of jazz."

Gerry Mulligan's music, said Bill Charlap, is "American music. Many of Gerry Mulligan's well-known songs are very singable. They could almost be in a show. Along with those very singable or diatonic sort of melodies, the harmony would have some of the angularity that gave it some of the rubs and the grease that sounded like jazz. 'Godchild' has got a lot going on because it's based on a song written by Harold Arlen, 'Between the Devil and the Deep Blue Sea.' I heard that for the first time when I was a fifteen-year-old kid, long before I thought I would ever be playing with Gerry Mulligan or anyone. The way Gerry Mulligan used ideas was completely unique. I figured something out about 'Rocker' recently. Typical of Gerry's mind is that he was always great with puns, he was great with anagrams. 'Rocker' was based on Leroy Anderson's 'Sleigh Ride.' That's Gerry's genius, to come up with something like that. It's not 'Sleigh Ride'; it's a new composition, and Gerry wrote his own harmonic terrain, using those Stravinsky ideas."

This, Charlap said, is where the composing, arranging, bandleading, and playing all came together. Mulligan, he explained, "knew the orchestra, knew the players, knew how to write for them. He had a complete understanding of the players. Like Ellington, he was a real arranger, the real thing. And he just loved leading a band—bandleader, bari player, composer, arranger, I think they're all equal. They're all part and parcel of each other. They can't exist without each other.

"By the time I was playing with Gerry," he continued, "I knew, 'Oh, wow, it's the great Gerry Mulligan.' I asked him if he would please write out the voicings for 'Godchild' because we weren't playing that material at the time. It was beautiful to watch him write it out. He wrote really small and meticulous. It was like a real writer. He was a completely unique figure. His music was very unique. He had a distinct melodic gift."

He was also, Newsom said, "So balanced in his contributions. Some people may like the *Birth of the Cool* and *Re-Birth of the Cool* better than they like *The Age of Steam* or some of his later work. I think it was his eminence in all those areas that made him what he was."

Larry Appelbaum believes Mulligan's name "still resonates today to anybody who's serious about jazz. The question for me is: What do people of today know of him? What do they associate? Is it the pianoless quartet stuff with Chet Baker? Is it the *Birth of the Cool* stuff with Miles? Is it his later big-band stuff? Is it his Concert Jazz Band stuff? If you just ask jazz fans, it might be one thing. If you ask musicians, it might be something else."

Improvisation is at the heart of jazz, and Mulligan was a master improviser. But there was a structure to his improvisation and his creativity. "He certainly had a gorgeous sound and played from the heart," said Rosenthal, but, "he was pretty intellectual in his approach. He was arranging, he was thinking, he was programming. That's one of the things I learned. To see how much organization or control he wanted to lay on top or be integral to what we were doing in every aspect—from the programming, to the order of the songs, to the order of the solos. He gave everything thought. I think he thought it was all deserving of serious attention. So that's the way he approached his music. There was a lot of structure to it. It wasn't, 'Let's go into a club and hang out and play whatever we feel like.'"

Although Smulyan never had the chance to play in a big band with Mulligan, "I know plenty of musicians who have," he said. "They said he was constantly revisiting music, rehearsing, adding things. He seemed very restless, musically. He was never satisfied with things being the status quo. He always seemed like he was tinkering. We spoke a few times, but we never shared the bandstand together. That's one of the regrets of my life."

Amram remembers Mulligan "sitting at the piano for hours, trying to get the right note. He would say, 'We know Stravinsky wrote in his book how sometimes he would play something fourteen times to get the correct harmony.' I said, 'Gerry, you're one of the masters of the choice notes.' Choice was an old African-American slang expression, meaning 'excellent,' 'beautiful,' 'of quality,' 'of the highest level.' The concept of choice notes not only meant that you'd find the most beautiful notes, but [also] that you had the ability and even the obligation to choose those notes and make something that happened as a result of your experience.

"Gerry was totally devoted to the music. He was very humble as far as the music went. He felt the music was a higher power. He never allowed himself to be manipulated. He kept developing, and he kept playing the saxophone better.

"I also loved to hear Gerry play the piano," Amram continued. "And the other thing that was unique about Gerry is that—with all the things he did—he was still able to maintain a sense of the swing era, the dance band era. And Dixieland, that sense of the New Orleans concept of everybody playing together. That almost disappeared when the intellectuals hung onto jazz and said, 'What's the next thing going to be?' Gerry never went for that. In a sense, he was a true old-fashioned artist. When he was a teenager he was a crazy little kid in love with music, and he never lost that. He's created a body of work that has lasting value and high standards that's yet to be appreciated."

Ted Nash acknowledged that when he joined Mulligan's band in 1980, "I still was in the place of being an impatient youngster. I appreciated what he did, but it didn't have a direct influence on me at the time. Now, I realize what a giant he was."

Mulligan, Nash continued, "loved music. He's in that category of Dizzy and people like that who just appreciated music for what it was. It didn't have to be a specific style. He just appreciated good music. His big-band arranging is as close to perfect as you can get."

During the years Ron Vincent played drums with Mulligan's groups, he knew he was "doing something really great. As time goes by and I listen to more older music, I realize just how incredible he was. I heard everything in his playing. When you listen to him and Brookmeyer together, there's all that counterpoint they did—right out of the tradition of Dixieland. And then you hear the crossover from Dixie to swing, which is where I think he lived. He was in that bit of time where things were crossing over into bebop. But he could hang with the best."

Vincent remembered a time when the quartet played with Wynton Marsalis. "Wynton is a very modern player. Gerry went, 'Oh, sure we can do that'—and bang! He was right there with him. He had the biggest musical ears. I've never been around someone who could hear things like that. He could hear it immediately and know what it was and say, 'No, no, I don't want that. I want this.' He had a real talent for in-the-moment arranging."

Recalling one night with Marsalis at New York's Town Hall, Mulligan said, "Wynton Marsalis and I did a counterpoint thing on a show of George Wein's. We just burned it out, we had such a great time." In *Listen: Gerry Mulligan*, Marsalis commented on their chemistry: "He could play this counterpoint really well. It's very hard to find horn players who could play like that—two horns that can invent melodies at the same time. Sometimes we would play together and, at the end of the tune, we'd look at each other and go, 'Ooh!' To get all of the rhythms interlocked, it just takes a certain feeling of music."

On January 28, 1996, John Snyder told the *Chicago Tribune*'s Reich about the admiration Mulligan had for Marsalis. "I wish I could have done something like Wynton is doing now when I was young," Mulligan told Snyder, "but I didn't have the patience for it, and I didn't have the personality."

Writing in the June 1996 issue of *Jazz Times*, Ira Gitler said Mulligan "always swung, and his introduction of contrapuntal lines was never precious, always organic."

Marsalis, in the *Listen: Gerry Mulligan* video, pointed out that Mulligan "was very, very meticulous. He wanted his music to be rehearsed in a certain way. He was very, very serious about music. A lot of times, when you're out there playing, the environment is not very conducive to being serious. Stuff's rushed, put together all in a hurry. Guys come in late. Gerry Mulligan—throughout his years in music, his belief in professionalism did not erode."

Mulligan detested music that became "so bloody serious and self-conscious—so terribly aware of its social importance—that it's just become pompous beyond enjoying it . . . It isn't a joy to hear some cat struggling for twenty or thirty minutes on a solo," he told me in 1981. He had previously expounded on this subject in the liner notes to *What Is There to Say*, a 1959 album reissued on the Sony label in 1994. "Jazz music," Mulligan said, "is fun to me. But some of the people who do the most talking about jazz don't seem to get any real fun out of listening to it. It seems to me that all the super-intellectualizing on the techniques of jazz and the lack of response to the emotion and meaning of jazz is spoiling the fun for listeners and players alike."

Also in 1959, Gunther Schuller told Nat Hentoff, in the March 21 *New Yorker* article, that Mulligan "has brought humor back into modern jazz. Jazz, which had been so happy a music in the '30s, had become quite serious, and even, at times, sickly, during the development of modern idioms. Mulligan brought back a happy, relaxed feeling because he is able to relax completely while playing."

Mulligan's "melodicism," said Rosenthal, "was second to none. I think that's an echo of his composing and arranging tendencies. He was playing melodies that he would sometimes end up writing down and make them his compositions. Some of his shout choruses for other people's tunes were very melodic, and he ended up using those as just being the compositions. He'd play those, and they'd become a Gerry Mulligan tune. Or, they started out being a little riff or a shout chorus on another song, much the way the bebop players would write new melodies over the old standards."

Another of Mulligan's pianists, Bill Mays, told me that "Gerry could play the simplest melody and make it mean something. His lyrical side was beautiful. Same with his writing. He structured each set very carefully, with great variety in terms of mood, tempo. But, even within the very specific order of the 'show,' there was the chance for lots of spontaneity."

Within the melodic framework, Gary Smulyan said, Mulligan "was constantly trying new things, trying to stretch the boundaries of what he knew and what he did. He was never really satisfied with being in the same place. That's the sign of a great musician."

"No musician in the post-bop era," wrote Gary Giddins, in *Visions of Jazz: The First Century*, "was more adept at crossing boundaries. Though a confirmed modernist credited with spreading the amorphous notion of cool jazz, he achieved some of this finest work in collaborations with his swing era idols, Ben Webster and Johnny Hodges; he displayed a photograph of Jack Teagarden in his studio. He was specially proud of appearing in the Billie Holiday segment in *The Sound of Jazz*—typically, the only modernist, the only white musician, the only improviser to play a double-time solo. The trumpet player Rex Stewart, who also appeared on that telecast, once compared the first time he heard Mulligan with the first time he heard Armstrong: 'I felt a kinship with him right away. If a man doesn't feel him, he must be dead.'"

Jersey Jazz writer Joe Lang, in March 1996, described Mulligan as "an innovator as a player, composer, arranger, leader, and catalyst. He combined an overwhelming talent with his innate intelligence, wit, and sense of style to produce some of his most memorable music of the last fifty years."

Elliott Lawrence believed Mulligan "could write anything he really wanted to. I'm sure he could have written a Broadway show, certainly better than a lot of Broadway show composers."

Brookmeyer and Rosenthal did a series of duo concerts together. During an interview after one of them, the interviewer asked Brookmeyer, "Who is the person you've collaborated with over the years that you have the most respect for?" Brookmeyer replied: "Gerry Mulligan."

To George Wein, Mulligan "was just one of the greatest jazz musicians I ever heard. He had all the traditions in his playing, but he was contemporary at the same time. A very rare thing. He's one of the all-stars of all-stars. He would be in anybody's first-string band." Added Smulyan: "One note, and you know it's him. You can't say that about a lot of people."

Afterword

I was too young to have witnessed the popularity of the Gerry Mulligan pianoless quartet. When the Concert Jazz Band was flourishing, I was in college, aware of the Brubeck Quartet, but, inexplicably, unaware of Mulligan. I became familiar with his recorded music in the mid-'60s but didn't see him live until the mid-1970s, starting with the Mulligan-Baker reunion concert at Carnegie Hall in 1974.

Not appreciating what a big star he had been in the '50s and early '60s, I was initially drawn to his recorded music simply because I liked it, but his live performances generated a special kind of musical energy. Even if you knew nothing about Mulligan, you sensed that you were seeing and hearing something extraordinary. It was the melodicism combined with the showmanship and outstanding musicianship that combined to make a Gerry Mulligan performance unforgettable. I saw him numerous times at Hopper's in Greenwich Village, taking my future wife, Linda, and hoping she'd like him and his music as much as I did. (She did.) We were at the Newport Jazz Festival in New York concert in 1979 when he surprised the audience with his new big band, instead of his quartet. That was a special evening. We also saw him and his quartet perform with Zubin Mehta and the New York Philharmonic in 1989 at Lincoln Center.

In 1981, I was doing some freelance writing for a publication called *ELECTRICity,* which was distributed on college campuses, music shops, and bookstores in the Philadelphia area. Gerry and Franca were appearing at J&R Music on Park Row in the Wall Street area to promote *Walk on the*

Water, and I took the subway downtown during my lunch hour to buy the album, have Gerry sign it for Linda, and to ask him if I could interview him for *ELECTRICity*. He not only agreed to the interview, but also invited me to come up to their home in Darien, which I did on a Saturday afternoon. It was a special day and a memory that I will always cherish. That interview also became the basis for a chapter in my previous book, *Jazz Notes: Interviews Across the Generations* (Praeger/ABC-Clio).

I would be hard-pressed to estimate the number of times I saw Gerry in concert at either Carnegie Hall or Lincoln Center, at Hopper's or StoryTowne on East 58th Street, at the Bottom Line, the South Street Seaport, or wherever he surfaced. Another particularly memorable night was a "Two Generations of Brubeck" concert at either Carnegie Hall or Avery Fisher Hall, I don't remember which. Dave Brubeck and his sons played in the first half, and the second half featured the Dave Brubeck Trio (Jack Six on bass, Alan Dawson on drums), with special guests Paul Desmond and Gerry Mulligan. If you saw Mulligan and Desmond walking down the street, you would never guess they had anything in common, but on the stage that night, they were *Two of a Mind*, to quote the title of one of their albums. Then, when the two concerts were finished, everyone came out for an encore, and, of course, Gerry took over as leader of the band. He was no longer the guest soloist. He was leading his own band again, extemporaneously, and enjoying it immensely.

I would give anything now to have been on that cruise in December 1995. Thank goodness for the CDs, iTunes, YouTube, and every other outlet that enables his music and his personal magnetism to live on. I contacted Franca in 2011 because I felt no one had yet written a book chronicling Gerry's enormous contributions to jazz and American music as a composer, arranger, bandleader, and musician. I feel blessed to have been able to see him in person as often as I did, and one of my hopes is that this book might introduce him to those who were not as fortunate . . . and rekindle some memories for those like me who wish we could see him again, one more time.

Sources

Books

Balliett, Whitney. 2000. *A Journal of Jazz 1954-2000*. New York: St. Martin's Press.

Crouch, Stanley. 2006. *Considering Genius*. New York: Civitas Books.

Dixon, Gail. 2004. *The Music of Harry Freedman*. Toronto: University of Toronto Press.

Gardner, Mark. 1991. *The Blackwell Guide to Recorded Jazz*. Hoboken, NJ: Wiley.

Gavin, James. 2002. *Deep in a Dream: The Long Night of Chet Baker*. New York: Alfred A. Knopf.

Giddins, Gary. 1998. *Visions of Jazz: The First Century*. Oxford, UK: Oxford University Press.

Gioia, Ted. 1992. *West Coast Jazz*. Oxford, UK: Oxford University Press.

Gordon, Max. 1980. *Live at the Village Vanguard*. New York: St. Martin's Press.

Gordon, Robert. 1986. *Jazz West Coast*. London: Quartet Books.

Hentoff, Nat. 1976. *Jazz Is*. New York: Random House.

Hershorn, Tad. 2011. *Norman Granz: The Man Who Used Jazz for Justice*. Oakland, CA: University of California Press.

Horricks, Raymond. 1986. *Gerry Mulligan's Ark*. London: Apollo Press Ltd.

Jack, Gordon. 2004. *Fifties Jazz Talk: An Oral Retrospective*. Lanham, MD: Scarecrow Press.

Josephson, Sanford. 2009. *Jazz Notes: Interviews Across the Generations*. Santa Barbara, CA: Praeger/ABC-Clio.

Klinkowitz, Jerome. 1991. *Listen: Gerry Mulligan—An Aural Narrative in Jazz*. New York: Schirmer Books.

Lees, Gene. 2000. *Arranging the Score: Portraits of the Great Arrangers*. London: Bloomsbury Publishing Plc.

Schuller, Gunther. 2011. *A Life in Pursuit of Music and Beauty*. Rochester, NY: University of Rochester Press.

Simon, George T. 1974. *The Big Bands.* New York: Collier Books.

Tirro, Frank. 2008. *The Birth of the Cool of Miles Davis and His Associates*. Hillsdale, NY: Pendragon Press.

Ward, Geoffrey C. and Ken Burns. 2000. *Jazz: A History of America's Music*. New York: Alfred A. Knopf.

Widener, Don. 1975. *Lemmon: A Biography*. New York: Macmillan.

Album and Program Notes

Carriere, Claude. Gerry Mulligan, *Paris Concert.* World Pacific WPL1016 (1966).

Cuscuna, Michael. Gerry Mulligan, *The Age of Steam*. A&M Records SP 3036 (1971).

Friedwald, Will. Claude Thornhill, *Best of Big Bands*. Sony (1991).

Hentoff, Nat. Gerry Mulligan and the Concert Jazz Band, *At the Village Vanguard.* Verve V-8396 (2002, originally recorded in 1960).

Kirschner, Bill. *The Complete Verve Gerry Mulligan Concert Jazz Band Sessions*. Mosaic (1960-62, out of print).

Milkowski, Bill. *Marian McPartland Plays the Music of Alec Wilder*. Halcyon HAL 109 (1974).

Milkowski, Bill. The Dave Brubeck Quartet Featuring Gerry Mulligan, *The Last Set at Newport.* Atlantic SD1607 (1972).

Mulligan, Gerry. *Dragonfly*. Telarc Jazz CD83377 (1995).

Pujol, Jordi. Gerry Mulligan and the Concert Jazz Band, *Santa Monica 1960*. Fresh Sound Records FSR 710 (2012).

Ramey, Philip. Israel Philharmonic program notes (1987).

Ramey, Philip. New York Philharmonic program notes (1989).

Sea Cliff Chamber Players program notes (1990).

Townsend, Irving. Duke Ellington and His Orchestra, *Newport 1958*. Columbia CL1245 (1958).

Articles, Periodicals, Blogs, and Papers

allaboutjazz.com, December 1, 2000.
amazon.co.uk
Bailey, C. Michael. allaboutjazz.com, September 15, 2010.
Berg, Chuck. *Down Beat*, May 1974
Birnbaum, Larry. *Down Beat*, January 1997.
Bourne, Michael. *Down Beat*, January 1989.
Chambers, Jack. *Coda*, September, 1976.
Chinen, Nate. *Jazz Times*, April 2004.
Cook, Richard. *Jazz Review*, October 2001.
Dryden, Ken. allmusic.com.
Eckert, Jr., Thor. *The Christian Science Monitor*, May 12, 1982.
Erlewin, Stephen Thomas. allmusic.com.
Feather, Leonard. *Down Beat*, May 1960.
Fine, Richard Samuel. *The Birth of Jeru: Gerry Mulligan's Early Composing/Arranging Career (1945-1953)*, 2010.
Franklin, David. *Jazz Times*, June 2003.
Friedwald, Will. jazz.com.
Fuller, Jack. *Chicago Tribune*, June 25, 1989.
Gitler, Ira. *Jazz Times*, June 1996.
Heckman, Don. *Los Angeles Times*, August 2, 2001; May 3, 2001; January 25, 1996.
Henahan, Donal. *The New York Times*, May 7, 1982.
Hentoff, Nat. *The New Yorker*, March 21, 1959.
Horricks, Raymond. *Crescendo & Jazz Music*, October 11, 1998; February 3, 1998; August 9, 1997.
Jack, Gordon. *Jazz Journal*, March 2002.
Jeske, Lee. *Down Beat*, April 1981.
Joyce, Mike. *Jazz Times*, October 2007.
Kendall, Ian. *Jazz Journal International*, February 1978.
Klee, Joe. *Down Beat*, May 1974.
Lang, Joe. *Jersey Jazz*, March 1996.

Lewis, David. *Coda*, January 2, 1998.
Lucraft, Howard. *Crescendo & Jazz Music*, February/March 1996.
McDonough, John. *Down Beat*, July 1988; April 1996.
Myers, Mark. jazzwax.com, November 15, 2011.
The New York Times
Pareles, Jon. *The New York Times*, June 30, 1992.
Ramsey, Doug. *Jazz Times*, June 2001; September 2000.
Reich, Howard. *Chicago Tribune*, January 22, 1996; January 28, 1996.
Roberts, Joel. allaboutjazz.com, November 1, 2002.
Rusch, Bob. *Cadence*, October, 1977.
Schudel, Matt. *Sun Sentinel*, February 4, 1996.
Simon, George. *New York Herald Tribune*, May 21, 1961.
Smith, Arnold Jay. *Down Beat*, July 1976.
Screen Archives Entertainment
Time, February 21, 1953.
Tognazzini, Anthony. allmusic.com.
Tucker, Mark. *The New York Times*, November 19, 1989.
Whitehead, Kevin. *Down Beat*, August 1992.
Wilkins, Woodrow. allaboutjazz.com, December 7, 2007.
Willard, Patricia. *Down Beat*, October 1974.
Wilson, John S. *The New York Times*, February 28, 1975.
Wilson, Russ. *Oakland Tribune*, April 1959.
Woods, Phil. *Saxophone Journal*, July/August 1996.
Woodward, Josef. *Jazz Times*, June 1998.
Yanow, Scott. allmusic.com.

Interviews

Gerry Mulligan—Darien, Connecticut: November 1981.
David Amram—Putnam Valley, New York: December 29, 2013.
Larry Appelbaum—Washington, D.C.: August 7, 2014.
Dave Bergeron—phone interview: September 3, 2014.
Ron Carter—phone interview: September 28, 2014.
Bill Charlap—West Orange, New Jersey: April 29, 2014.
Bill Crow—New City, New York: April 9, 2013.
Claire Daly—phone interview: February 4, 2014.

Harold Danko—phone interview: August 18, 2014.
Rich DeRosa—phone interview: June 19, 2014.
Mitch Forman—phone interview: August 30, 2014.
Tom Harrell—phone interview: September 26, 2014.
Ted Hogarth—phone interview: October 4, 2014.
Bill Holman—phone interview: May 20, 2014.
Dean Johnson—phone interview: June 7, 2014.
Elliot Lawrence—phone interview: October 23, 2012.
Julian Lee—phone interview: August 8, 2014.
Dick Lowenthal—phone interview: September 26, 2014.
Frank Luther—Woodstock, New York: July 27, 2014.
Johnny Mandel—phone interview: March 3, 2014.
Bill Mays—email interview: October 26, 2014.
John McNeil—phone interview: November 17, 2013.
Zubin Mehta—phone interview: October 18, 2014.
Franca Mulligan—Darien, Connecticut: June 18, 2014.
Ted Nash—New York, New York: November 13, 2013.
Jon Newsom—phone interview: August 11, 2014.
Keith O'Quinn—phone interview: February 8, 2014.
Lisa Parrott—phone interview: September 25, 2014.
Leigh Pilzer—phone interview: January 2, 2014.
Alan Raph —phone interviews: July 21, 2014; September 1, 2014.
Scott Robinson—New York, New York: August 31, 2013.
Wallace Roney—phone interview: October 19, 2014.
Ted Rosenthal—phone interview: September 10, 2014.
Loras Schissel—Washington, DC: August 7, 2014.
John Scofield—phone interview: November 2, 2014.
Lauren Sevian—phone interview: February 6, 2014.
Jack Six—phone interview: October 12, 2014.
Gary Smulyan—New York, New York: July 10, 2014.
Warren Vaché—phone interview: August 16, 2014.
Ron Vincent—Manalapan, New Jersey: October 6, 2013.
George Wein—New York, New York: June 19, 2013.
Phil Woods—Delaware Water Gap, Pennsylvania: March 8, 2014.

Discography

For a full discography of Gerry Mulligan's works, please visit www.gerrymulligan.com.

1951

Conception (Original Jazz Classics)
Gerry Mulligan Blows (Prestige)
Historically Speaking (Prestige)
Mulligan Plays Mulligan (Original Jazz Classics)

1952

Gerry Mulligan Quartet (Pacific Jazz)

1953

Gerry Mulligan and His Ten-tette (Capitol Records)
Gerry Mulligan Quartet, Vol. 1 (Pacific Jazz)
Gerry Mulligan Quartet, Vol. 2 (Pacific Jazz)
Konitz Meets Mulligan (EMI/Pacific Jazz)
Lee Konitz Plays with the Gerry Mulligan Quartet (Pacific Jazz)
Revelation (Blue Note)
The Original Gerry Mulligan Tentet and Quartet (GNP/Crescendo)

1954

California Concerts (World Pacific)
California Concerts, Vol. 1 (Pacific Jazz)
California Concerts, Vol. 2 (Pacific Jazz)
California Concerts, Vols. 1 & 2 (Toshiba EMI)
Gerry Mulligan in Paris, Vol. 1 (RCA)
Gerry Mulligan in Paris, Vol. 2 (RCA)
Gerry Mulligan with Paul Chambers (Original Jazz Classics)
Lee Konitz and the Gerry Mulligan Quartet (Chameleon)
Paris Concert (Pacific Jazz)
Pleyel Concert (Vogue)

1955

Presenting the Gerry Mulligan Sextet (Membran)
Presenting the Sextet (Emarcy)

1956

At Storyville (Pacific Jazz)
Gerry Mulligan Quartet/Paul Desmond Quintet (Original Jazz Classics/Fantasy)
Mainstream of Jazz (Emarcy)

1957

Birth of the Cool (Capitol Records)
Desmond Meets Mulligan (Verve)
Gerry Mulligan Meets Stan Getz (Verve)
Gerry Mulligan & Paul Desmond Quartet (Verve/Polygram)
Getz Meets Mulligan in Hi-Fi (Verve/Polygram)
Lee Konitz with the Gerry Mulligan Quartet (Pacific Jazz)
Live in Stockholm (Moon)
Mulligan Meets Monk (Origin Records/Original Jazz Classics)
Reunion with Chet Baker (Blue Note/EMI-Manhattan)
Songbook (Blue Note)
The Mulligan Songbook (Blue Note)

1958

I Want to Live (Jazz Plaza Music)

1959

Gerry Mulligan Meets Ben Webster (Verve/Polygram)
The New Gerry Mulligan Quartet (Tax)
What Is There to Say? (Legacy/Sony Music Distribution)

1960

A Profile of Gerry Mulligan (Universal Distribution)
Gerry Mulligan Meets Johnny Hodges (Verve)
Nightwatch (United Artists Records)
The Genius of Gerry Mulligan (Pacific Jazz Records)
The Gerry Mulligan Concert Jazz Band on Tour (Verve)

1961

A Concert in Jazz (Verve)
Dizzy Gillespie/Gerry Mulligan (Europa)
Gerry Mulligan and the Concert Jazz Band (Verve)
Gerry Mulligan and the Concert Jazz Band at the Village Vanguard (Verve)
Gerry Mulligan Presents a Concert in Jazz (Verve)

1962

Gerry Mulligan and His Quartet (Laserlight)
Jeru (Legacy/Sony Music Distribution)
The Gerry Mulligan Quartet (Verve)
Two of a Mind (Bluebird RCA)

1963

Gerry Mulligan '63: The Concert Jazz Band (Universal Japan)
Night Lights (Verve)
Spring Is Sprung (Philips)
Timeless (Pacific Jazz)

1965

Butterfly with Hiccups (Limelight Records)
Mulligan-Baker (Fantasy)

1966

Concert Days (Sunset Records)
Feelin' Good (Limelight)
Gerry Mulligan With Guest Soloist Zoot Sims (I Giganti Del Jazz)
If You Can't Beat 'Em, Join 'Em (Limelight Records)
Something Borrowed, Something Blue (Limelight Records)

1968

Compadres (with Dave Brubeck Trio, CBS)

1969

Blues Roots (with Dave Brubeck Trio, CBS)
Jazz Fest Masters (Scotti Brothers)

1971

The Age of Steam (A&M)

1972

We're All Together For The First Time (with Dave Brubeck, Paul Desmond, Atlantic)

1973

Live at the Berlin Philharmonic (with Dave Brubeck Trio, Columbia)

1974

Carnegie Hall Concert (Master Sound/Legacy)
Carnegie Hall Concert, Vol. 2 (CTI Records)

Gerry Mulligan/Astor Piazzolla (M10)
Summit – Reunion Cumbre (ANS)

1975

Gerry Mulligan Meets Enrico Intra (Pausa Records)

1976

Idol Gossip (Chiaroscuro)

1977

Lionel Hampton Presents Gerry Mulligan (Who's Who in Jazz)

1980

Holliday with Mulligan (DRG)
Walk on the Water (DRG)

1982

La Menace (DRG)

1983

Little Big Horn (GRP)

1984

Paradise Café (with Barry Manilow, Arista)

1986

Soft Lights & Sweet Music (Concord Jazz)

1987

Symphonic Dreams (Akustik)

1989

Lonesome Boulevard (A&M)

1991

Moonlight in Vermont (Candid)
The Best of the Gerry Mulligan Quartet with Chet Baker (Pacific Jazz/Capitol Records)

1992

Re-Birth of the Cool (GRP)

1993

Billy Taylor & Gerry Mulligan Live at MCG (Telarc)
In Concert (JVC Compact Discs)
Paraiso: Jazz Brazil (Telarc)

1994

Dream a Little Dream (Telarc)

1995

Dragon Fly (Telarc)

2000

Theme for Jobim: Gitanes Jazz (Polygram)

2003

Midas Touch: Live in Berlin (Concord Jazz)

2005

The Classic Concert Live (Concord Jazz)

2006

At the Village Vanguard (Poll Winners Records)
Gerry Mulligan Sextet (Membran)
Mosaic Select Gerry Mulligan (Mosaic)
On Tour/Jazz Soloist: Zoot Sims (Doxy Records)
Relax! (Wax Time)
The Lady is a Tramp (Fourmatt)
Western Reunion (Music Center)
Zurich 1962 Swiss Radio Days Jazz Series, Vol. 9 (TCB Records)

Index

Grateful acknowledgment is made to the following for permission to use published materials.

Bloomsbury Publishing PLC: Excerpt from *Arranging the Score: Portraits of the Great Arrangers*, by Gene Lees, © Gene Lees, 2000, Continuum, an imprint of Bloomsbury Publishing PLC.

Samuel R. Fine. *The Birth of Jeru: Gerry Mulligan's Early Composing/Arranging Career (1945–1953)*. Ph.D. dissertation: University of Maryland, 2010.

Jordi Pujol. Liner notes from the CD *Gerry Mulligan and the Concert Jazz Band: Santa Monica 1960* (Fresh Sound FSR 710).

South Florida Sun-Sentinel. Excerpt from article published in the *Sun-Sentinel* on February 4, 1996 ("Cool Jazz Revival," by Matt Schudel) used with permission of the *South Florida Sun-Sentinel*, © 2015. No endorsement by the *Sun-Sentinel* is made or implied.

Bob Rusch. Excerpt from article published in *Cadence* ©1977.

Frank Alkyer. Excerpts from three *Down Beat* articles. 1/89 by Michael Bourne, 10/74 by Patricia Willard, and 7/76 by Arnold Jay Smith.

Jazz Times Magazine. Excerpts from two articles. "Gerry Mulligan 1927–1996," by Ira Gitler (June 1996), and "Gerry Mulligan Midas Touch: Live in Berlin," by David Franklin (June 2003).

Estate of Mark Tucker. Excerpt from an article published in *The New York Times* on November 19, 1989.

Oxford University Press, USA. Excerpt from *Visions of Jazz: The First Century* by Gary Giddins (Oxford University Press, 1998), 328w from pp. 356, 358-359.

The Christian Science Monitor. Excerpt from an article by Thor Eckert Jr. Excerpted with permission from the May 12, 1982 issue of *The Christian Science Monitor*. © 1982 The Christian Science Monitor (www.csmonitor.com).

David Winkler. Excerpt from program notes of the Sea Cliff Players Concert of April 1990. Herbert Sucoff, founder, the Sea Cliff Chamber Players.

Rowman & Littlefield. Excerpt from *Fifties Jazz Talk: An Oral Retrospective*, by Gordon Jack (Scarecrow Press).